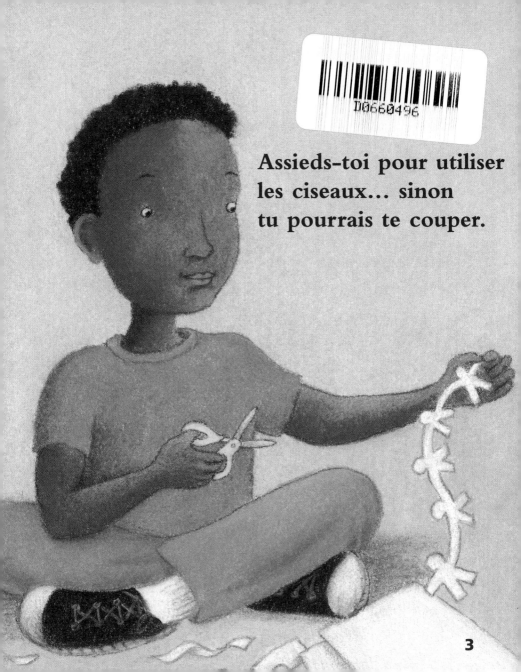

Assieds-toi pour utiliser
les ciseaux... sinon
tu pourrais te couper.

**Lave-toi les mains avant le repas...
sinon tu pourrais manger
de la saleté!**

Demande avant de goûter...
sinon tu pourrais
t'empoisonner.

6

**Regarde avant de toucher...
sinon tu pourrais te tacher!**

Reste avec une grande personne… sinon tu pourrais t'égarer.

Assieds-toi bien droit
sur ta chaise... sinon
tu pourrais en tomber!

Accroche-toi lorsque
tu grimpes… sinon
tu pourrais chuter.

Attache bien ton manteau...
sinon tu pourrais
t'enrhumer.

Demande avant de flatter...
sinon tu pourrais te faire
attaquer.

Attache tes lacets...
sinon tu pourrais trébucher.

À vélo, n'oublie pas ton casque…
sinon tu pourrais t'assommer.

Boucle ta ceinture
de sécurité... sinon
tu pourrais te blesser.

Sois toujours prudent...

dans chacune
de tes activités.

Rien n'est plus important
que ta sécurité.

LISTE DE MOTS

à	dans	les	sinon
accroche	de	lorsque	sois
activités	demande	mains	sur
assieds	droit	manger	ta
assommer	égarer	manteau	tacher
attache	empoisonner	oublie	te
attaquer	en	pas	tes
avant	enrhumer	personne	toi
avec	est	plus	tomber
bien	faire	pour	ton
blesser	flatter	pourrais	toucher
boucle	goûter	prudent	toujours
casque	grande	que	trébucher
ceinture	grimpes	regarde	tu
chacune	important	repas	une
chaise	la	reste	utiliser
chuter	lacets	rien	vélo
ciseaux	lave	saleté	
couper	le	sécurité	

À mes collègues enseignants qui travaillent si fort
pour la sécurité des enfants
— K.S.

Pour Julia et Rachel
— K.P.

Catalogage avant publication de
Bibliothèque et Archives Canada

Schulz, Kathy
Fais bien attention! / Kathy Schulz;
illustrations de Katherine Potter;
texte français de Caroline Ricard.

(Apprentis lecteurs)

Traduction de : Always Be Safe.
Pour les 3-6 ans.
ISBN 0-439-94797-9

I. Potter, Katherine II. Ricard, Caroline, 1978-
III. Titre. IV. Collection.

PZ23.S534Fa 2005   j813'.54   C2005-904336-9

Édition publiée par les Éditions Scholastic, 604, rue King Ouest, Toronto (Ontario) M5V 1E1.

6 5 4 3 2   Imprimé au Canada   07 08 09 10

FAIS BIEN ATTENTION!

Kathy Schulz
Illustrations de Katherine Potter

Texte français de Caroline Ricard

Éditions
SCHOLASTIC

ALAN AYCKBOURN

Confusions

Five interlinked one-act plays

With a Commentary and Notes by
RUSSELL WHITELEY

Methuen Student Editions
METHUEN DRAMA

Methuen Student Edition
This Methuen Student Edition first published in 1983
by Methuen London Ltd

11 12 10

Reissued with a new cover design 1994

Methuen Publishing Limited
215 Vauxhall Bridge Road, London SW1V 1EJ

Methuen Publishing Limited Reg. No. 3543167

Confusions first published as an acting edition only by Samuel
French Ltd, London, in 1977. The text of this Methuen edition
is off-set from the Samuel French edition by permission.

ISBN 0 413 532 704

Front cover photograph shows Pauline Collins as Polly
(Photo: John Haynes)

Printed and bound in Great Britain by
Cox & Wyman Ltd, Reading, Berkshire

*Special thanks are due to Alan Ayckbourn and Malcolm Page
for help in the preparation of this edition.*

Contents

Photos (by John Haynes) of the London premiere production appear on pages iv, xxiv-xxviii and xxx as well as on the front cover.

Between Mouthfuls: Martin, Polly and the Waiter

Alan Ayckbourn

Alan Ayckbourn was born in 1939 in Hampstead and attended Haileybury, a public school. When a young man he joined Donald Wolfit's company as an assistant stage manager (ASM) after which he went to the Connaught Theatre, Worthing, for six months as a student ASM. He followed this with a spell as ASM and actor at Leatherhead and shortly afterwards joined the Stephen Joseph Library Theatre in the Round in Scarborough as resident Stage Manager. In his first season there he acted in *An Inspector Calls* then moved on to Oxford Playhouse as ASM and actor.

In 1957 he returned to Scarborough and with Stephen Joseph's company went on tour to Leicester, Hemel Hempstead, Harlow and Newcastle-under-Lyme. In the winter of 1958-59 he wrote *The Square Cat* for himself and the company. This was followed by *Love After All*, which the company played in its 1959-60 winter season in Scarborough. Both those plays were written under the name of Roland Allen.

He then joined the RAF in Bedfordshire for two days in January 1960 before returning, yet again, to Scarborough as stage manager. As a member of the Stephen Joseph Studio Theatre Company he became a founder member of the company which came to be established at the Victoria Theatre, Stoke-on-Trent, where he remained for eighteen months. He wrote *Mr. Whatnot* for the Stoke company in 1963 but left in 1964 when, under the management of Peter Bridge, the play was presented at the Arts Theatre in London. This year also saw his last appearance as an actor in a production of *Two for the Seesaw* performed in Rotherham with Heather Stoney.

He went to the BBC in Leeds as a radio drama producer in 1964 and stayed there until 1970. During this time he continued to write and direct for summer seasons at the Theatre-in-the-round in Scarborough and in 1970 he took over as director of productions.

From this date the awards began pouring in. In 1973 he won the Evening Standard Best Comedy Award for *Absurd Person Singular* and followed this in 1974 with the Evening Standard *and* Plays and Players Best Play Awards and a US Emmy nomination for the Best

Comedy Series for *The Norman Conquests*. Also in this year he was voted Playwright of the Year by the Variety Club of Great Britain for *Absurd Person Singular* and *The Norman Conquests*.

In 1976 he moved the Scarborough company out of its fit-up home in the town's library into its own permanent theatre (subsequently re-named the Stephen Joseph Theatre-in-the-Round) in a converted school.

1977 saw another Best Play Award from The Standard for *Just Between Ourselves* followed by a Tony nomination for Best Play in 1979 for *Bedroom Farce*, the production from the National Theatre which transferred to Broadway. Also in that year *Joking Apart* shared the Plays and Players Best Comedy Award.

Subsequently Alan Ayckbourn has directed *Sisterly Feelings* at the National Theatre in 1980 and *Way Upstream* in 1982.

In 1981 he was made an Honorary D. Litt. of Hull University.

With Paul Todd as composer, he has written two late-night, five lunchtime and two full-length musical shows.

Ayckbourn's 1982 play for Scarborough, *Intimate Exchanges*, showed his continuing interest in deliberately complicated structure: it has two actors playing ten characters in a play which has two alternative first scenes, four alternative second scenes, eight alternative third scenes and sixteen possible fourth scenes.

Stage plays

The Square Cat (as Roland Allen): Scarborough, 1959.

Love After All (as Roland Allen): Scarborough, 1959.

Dad's Tale (as Roland Allen): Scarborough, 1960.

Standing Room Only (as Roland Allen): Scarborough, 1961.

Xmas v. Mastermind Victoria Theatre, Stoke-on-Trent 1962.

Mr Whatnot Stoke, 1963. London (Arts Theatre), 1964.

Meet My Father (re-titled *Relatively Speaking*) Scarborough,
    1965. London (Duke of York's), 1967.

The Sparrow Scarborough, 1967.

How the Other Half Loves Scarborough 1969. London (Lyric),
    1970. New York (Royale), 1971.

Me Times Me Times Me Scarborough, 1970. As *Family Circles:*
    (Richmond (Orange Tree), 1978.

Time and Time Again Scarborough, 1971. London (Comedy),
    1972.

Absurd Person Singular Scarborough, 1972. London (Criterion),
    1973. New York (Music Box), 1974.

The Norman Conquests Scarborough 1973. London (Globe), 1974.
New York (Morosco), 1975.

Absent Friends Scarborough 1974. London (Garrick), 1975.

Jeeves (musical with Andrew Lloyd Webber): London (Her
Majesty's), 1975.

Confusions Scarborough 1974. London (Apollo), 1976.

Bedroom Farce Scarborough 1975. London (National), 1977.

Just Between Ourselves Scarborough 1976. London (Queen's),
1977.

Ten Times Table Scarborough 1977. London (Globe), 1978.

Joking Apart: Scarborough 1978. London (Globe), 1979.

Men on Women on Men (late-night musical revue with Paul Todd)
Scarborough 1978.

Sisterly Feelings Scarborough, 1979, London (National), 1980.

Taking Steps Scarborough, 1979. London (Lyric), 1980.

Suburban Strains (with Paul Todd) Scarborough, 1980. London
(Round House), 1981.

First Course (Lunchtime musical entertainment with Paul Todd)
Scarborough, 1980.

Second Helping (lunchtime musical entertainment with Paul Todd)
Scarborough, 1980.

Season's Greetings Scarborough 1980. London (Apollo), 1982.

Me, Myself and I (lunchtime musical entertainment with Paul
Todd) Scarborough, 1981.

Way Upstream Scarborough, 1981. London (National), 1982.

Making Tracks (musical with Paul Todd) Scarborough, 1981.
Greenwich, 1983.

Intimate Exchanges Scarborough, 1982.

Incidental Music (musical entertainment with Paul Todd)
Scarborough 1983.

Television play
Service Not Included: BBC-TV, 1974.

Children's play
Ernie's Incredible Illucinations, 1969.

Commentary

Alan Ayckbourn believes that a playwright is essentially a craftsman. He differs from other writers in that his words are written to be used by other artists. As a craftsman, a playwright must serve his apprenticeship and master certain skills. Particularly important in Ayckbourn's philosophy are the shaping of a plot, scene or act and the expression of a character through words.

In his early career he spent much time observing and studying examples of the 'well-made play' as well as acknowledged classic pieces both ancient and modern. As part of his apprenticeship he wrote plays for himself as an actor, structuring these vehicles to show off his acting to its best advantage. He freely admits that his improvement as a writer was more rapid than his development as an actor, and he had to come to terms with the fact that he was not good enough to perform in his own plays.

Thus he made the conscious decision to become a writer/director, in which role he feels his interpretive and communicative powers are at their strongest. He is still very much an actors' playwright creating a showcase for their talents, and, by combining this with an astute eye for what is commercially successful in the theatre, he can almost guarantee the exposure of these talents to a wide audience.

Often criticised for this, Ayckbourn remains unashamedly devoted to the 'theatricality' of theatre – very much as Shakespeare was in his day. It is through this medium that he feels he is best able to make his statements about the human condition to a very large section of the theatre-going public. To Alan Ayckbourn there is no confusion between enlightenment and entertainment. In his work the two fuse together, and after a performance of one of his plays we leave the theatre content in the knowledge that we have witnessed a craftsman at work, we have laughed a great deal and at the same time we have become more informed about our own foibles and attitudes.

Ayckbourn is essentially a chronicler and editor of human behaviour. He juxtaposes the thoughts and dialogue of his characters in order to portray a faithful record of their lives. This is not a random exercise but the end product of a process of sensitive selection on his part. We are invited to become eavesdroppers on people and situations which are carefully orchestrated with delicate theatrical ingenuity. These painstakingly created suburban problems displayed on the stage for our benefit thus take on a greater significance. They become capable of being transformed into symbols of universal insecurities and anxieties. They are Hamlet's 'mirror held up to nature' reflecting, through comedy and farce, the often tragic undertones of our contemporary society.

In *Confusions* we can clearly see the craftsman at work. This set of five interlinked one-act plays, written originally to be played by five actors — three men and two women — ranges through naturalism, stylisation and into farce. However, underlying the comedy is the human dilemma of loneliness. This basic desire for companionship and the need to be accepted assume various guises within the plays themselves. There is the recurring theme of marital conflict as well as attacks on cant and hypocrisy which often lead ourselves and others into isolation. Self-delusion is also exposed as a contributor to our solitude. It would appear that none of us is safe.

On the surface the situations may appear inconsequential;

1. A mother unable to escape from baby talk.
2. An unsuccessful seduction attempt.
3. A fate-fraught dinner encounter.
4. A disastrous Garden Party.
5. A group of self-sacrificial characters on park benches.

Nevertheless our sympathy goes out to the characters, many of whom are misunderstood and oppressed, as we begin to appreciate the reasons behind their predicaments and recognise their cries for help.

Mother Figure

This play, the first of the five to be written, underlines in a masterly way the utter desolation which must overwhelm any harassed mum from time to time. With the craftsman's eye the situation is heightened and extended to include a couple of other unwary victims. Thus we get two for the price of one. The mother who deliberately, it appears, isolates herself from the outside world and can only communicate through the language of infancy; and the married couple who are also moving into isolation from each other. Lucy as well as Rosemary and her husband are victims of circumstance. The tragedy is that the life-lines which remain available are becoming ignored. Lucy cannot or will not answer the phone calls from her husband, and the next-door neighbours have long since abandoned any purposeful form of communication.

The comedy in this piece, if handled sensitively, underlines the pathos of both situations and helps to bring into sharp focus the process of gradual disintegration which is unfolding before us. The play calls for great sincerity in performance so as faithfully to portray Ayckbourn's characters and dialogue. The more matter-of-fact the situation appears the more venomous is the sting in the tail.

From the very opening of the play we are given an indication of what is to come. The frenetic running around after the children, the baby talk, the visual image of the untidy, dressing-gowned, unprepossessing housewife tearing great lengths of paper from a toilet roll all set the scene for us with great immediacy. We do not yet understand the significance of the ringing telephone but the automatic lifting — in passing — of the receiver and its instant replacement should give us some clue as to the lady's state of mind.

Into this world of semi-chaos creeps the frail, mousey-looking Rosemary, The entrance should almost hint at the fly insinuating itself into the spider's web. The fact that Rosemary is created as one of life's colourless, empty-headed creatures makes her role as a sacrificial lamb easily acceptable.

The beginning of their scene should move along fairly swiftly as the small talk is exchanged but then it leads into the significant line, 'I didn't get dressed today, that's all', which, if presented as just another piece of information within the conversation, gives it great pathetic strength. Lucy is not looking for sympathy. To her, not going out or not getting dressed are merely facts of life which she has come to accept. We, as observers, experience the shock and so become involved in her plight since she seems unable to grasp its significance herself. Any attempt by the actress at this stage to play overtly on our compassion would be almost bound to alienate us from the character.

We have just begun to take Lucy to our hearts when Rosemary, gaining in courage, begins to 'prattle on' about her role as neighbour. We see her at one point implying criticism, then immediately retracting it. Her insecurity causes her to vacillate, but once she is wound up and launched the words come spilling out. She desperately needs someone with whom she can communicate. The speech about the telephone call, played almost entirely on one breath, allows the floodgates to open fully. There seems to be genuine concern coming through but even Rosemary notices that she is gradually becoming ignored as Lucy's over-developed mothering instinct takes over.

However there is a point of contact where one feels, with some relief, that a form of acceptable exchange is going to take place, but this is soon over and is concluded with the placing of the telephone number on the table. Once Lucy offers a drink to her neighbour, by which gesture she is placing herself in the role of provider, the mother figure begins to reign supreme. Rosemary is obviously expecting something alcoholic rather than the orange or lemon on offer and from this moment she is to sink deeper into the infantile role in which Lucy has cast her.

For a while we are given a brief respite. Terry's entrance brings the play back onto a 'normal' plane and we feel that perhaps help is at hand. However, by now Lucy is well entrenched in her maternal character and reacts automatically to this other 'child' who has been inflicted upon her. Her tidying up and patronising of Terry and his wife brings out the male chauvinist in him and, through his nervousness at being subjected to this somewhat surreal treatment, we are given glimpses of the underlying reasons behind the parlous state of his marriage. The bickering which ensues between Rosemary and her husband – despite the adult language in which it is couched – has a well-observed childlike quality about it as, unwittingly, they fall under Lucy's spell.

From this moment on the situation deteriorates. Lucy is able to indulge herself by 'loving little Rosemary better' and using the well-worn device of Mr. Poddle to dispel the despair which her next-door neighbour is obviously experiencing.

The following episode, concerning the forgotten key is a clever piece of writing, exploding from the page as Terry becomes more frustrated with every sentence, Rosemary hides behind her new found ally and Lucy indulges to the hilt her 'mother as arbiter' function. The neighbours' regression is almost complete by now, manifesting itself in Rosemary sticking her tongue out at Terry and he being caught in the act of striking her. When they leave hand in hand, the transformation is total. We are horrified by the power which Lucy has developed within herself. Her complete absorption into the mother figure of the title, although it has given us some very amusing moments, gives us also cause of concern. Her personality has developed in such a way that its power to manipulate everyone and everything around her is reaching terrifying proportions.

Ayckbourn cleverly leaves Lucy muttering 'Blooming kids. Honestly' to soften the blow. It is a sentiment full of resignation and without malice, yet we have witnessed the almost Svengali-like influence which this woman can wield. Is she benign? Has the situation in which she finds herself led her inadvertently to discover a new form of theraphy? Does her natural instinct to 'mother' or 'smother' everyone around her hold some sinister meaning?

Whatever the answers to these questions the play is a salutary lesson to us all. It has a frightening realism about it which relays its message of 'there but for the grace of God go I'. It does not need overplaying. Its very simplicity is its strength; if the actors tackle it in an unaffected way following its patterns of light and shade faithfully it can have tremendous impact on an audience.

We are brought back to earth with a bump in Harry's telephone box soliloquy which gives us time to get our breath back and leads us into the much less complicated play which is to follow.

Drinking Companion

Here we are to meet Lucy's absentee husband. Harry, the father of her children, is revealed as merely that and nothing more. As with Terry and Rosemary we realise that for Harry and his wife marriage is a sham, marked by neglect and the breakdown of communication. Although a pathetic figure, trapped by his own inadequacy, Harry fails to gain our sympathy.

Despite the fact that when we first meet him within this play he has just returned from unsuccessfully telephoning Lucy, we do not warm to him. He is to spend the next twenty minutes or so demonstrating his ineptitude at seduction and incurring our malicious delight at his total failure. He is one of life's losers. The most distressing feature of the situation, in our eyes, is that because of *his* inability to cope he is dragging his wife down the same road.

This play, which Alan Ayckbourn contends is based on a real-life, observed situation, takes a sideways glance at both loneliness and boredom. Paula and Bernice who are to be 'entertained', wined and also dined, if the opportunity presents itself, must pay the price for their parasitic activities. They must sit there listening to the same stories and re-living the same situations night after night. Like the masochists they are this will be repeated the length and breadth of the country as their self-inflicted treadmill turns relentlessly throughout the year.

As the play opens Harry returns to continue 'chatting up' Paula and to his unfinished whisky and soda. Presumably he has had earlier drinks and during the course of the play he is to consume three more doubles. His progression into 'blundering' drunkeness must be carefully controlled since there are many long speeches to get through; as more whisky goes down, his dialogue and behaviour should become more outrageous. The actor playing Harry must carefully pace himself; in this he is skilfully guided by the play's construction. The part is a delight for an actor, testing as it does both his vocal capacity and bodily control.

The opening speeches with Harry being deliberately evasive about his family commitments and his cliché-ridden technique alienates us from the character enabling us to view the situation very much as outsiders. We can appreciate how hard he is having to work, desperately trying to keep the conversation going despite Paula's monsyllabic responses. After a process of 'softening up' Harry gets down to business. His comparison of Paula to a 'modern girl' and the 'modelling' inferences are loaded with sexual innuendo and he is careful at this point to announce his room number. From now onwards his single-mindedness is clearly demonstrated. The short staccato dialogue during which he discovers Paula's age and whether she has a boyfriend is masterly and builds beautifully into the promiscuity speech. Even during her protestations of innocence Paula is careful to leave the door slightly ajar. Her reply of 'Possibly' to Harry's direct questions on her sleeping around ensures that the supply of drinks will not dry up and, as we see from Harry's response, she is successful. It is significant that at this point Paula has to re-open the conversation which eight lines later grinds to a halt. She is by no means as experienced as Harry and to some extent gains our sympathy.

The would-be Casanova is by now convinced that a conquest is within his grasp. Relentlessly he returns to his former subject. The alcohol is loosening him up and his confidence bounces along. He is tying Paula in knots, and her rather inadequate attempts at parrying his attacks are speedily dealth with.

After the next pause Harry moves in for the kill. The double bed, the vodka and night of unbridled pleasure are unceremoniously offered. Fortunately for Paula, Ayckbourn, realising that the play is moving a little too quickly in this one direction, stages the 'Relief of Mafeking'. Bernice is seen in the Saloon Bar and the day is saved. Both actors and audience are offered the opportunity to get their breath back in preparation for the next instalment.

Bernice, the older and more experienced of the two girls, sweeps in and for the first time Harry finds himself pushed into the background. On this occasion he goes for the drinks himself rather than use the services of the waiter. He needs time to pull himself together since even he has realised that Bernice will be a much tougher nut to crack. This is borne out during the dialogue between the girls. Bernice, the old hand at the game, is hard and cynical. The excuse to leave is readily available and one almost feels, as she liberally douses herself with scent, that she is girding her loins to deal the 'coup de grace' to poor old Harry. Indeed she is to prove a formidable opponent.

On Harry's return, fortified no doubt with another 'swift one' to bolster his courage, it is Bernice who provides most of the responses. She slips easily into the lie propagated by Paula and proves that she is more than a match for Harry's particular brand of 'chat'. (Note the colour chosen by Harry for Bernice: 'Ice Blue', which sums up her character perfectly.) Her 'You never know your luck, do you?' begins a chain reaction which puts Harry on the defensive and signals the beginning of the end.

His brain is becoming fuddled now. He is confused and losing the ability to cope. His tone is almost pleading, and when he blunders into the 'wife doesn't understand me' speech we get a glimpse of the real Harry. The problems he will not face are paraded before us as the alcohol begins to take him over. He is now desperate and belligerent as he sees his opportunity slipping away. Like a drowning man he is clutching at straws as he bandies his room number around yet again and finally throws down the gauntlet in the guise of his key. His words are slurred and his movement unco-ordinated. He crumbles before our eyes while Bernice impassively walks all over him in her desire to get away. Paula tries to soften the blows for Harry's sake but she too is subservient to Bernice's wishes and personality. It is devastation. Within the space of ten minutes Harry is destroyed.

As he stumbles out of the bar to secure a taxi for the girls he is in full retreat. He cannot resist a final piece of flattery which makes us squirm in our seats, and his 'Wait there' is a parting shot of bravado which we are all convinced will be ignored. The girls' exit with the waiter retrieving the key is the ultimate humiliation for Harry. The waiter has seen it all before and as the key slips into his back pocket the curtain mercifully falls on the whole unsavoury incident.

The comedy in this particular play does not have the same bitter edge to it that it has in *Mother Figure*. Pathetic it may be, but we remain detached from the basic situation. We do not want Harry to succeed and thus we are able to enjoy the humour of the failure so much more. We revel in the cat-and-mouse game which is being played. There is almost a verbal 'Tom and Jerry' feel to the play as it builds to its somewhat frantic climax. Because of this it requires careful handling and deliberate pacing. Small climaxes are created then allowed to fall away as the build up to the next one begins. The characters and dialogue complementing each other to provide the contrasts in pace, mood and activity which the play demands. More overtly 'theatrical' than the first piece it leads skilfully into *Between Mouthfuls*, where we are to see the devices of theatre being paraded before us.

Between Mouthfuls

In this play Ayckbourn uses the theatrical cliché to great effect. There are two troubled marriages, a ruthless adulterous businessman and his nagging wife teamed up with a young, ambitious workaholic whose wife has sought consolation elsewhere. To this quartet is added a human catalyst in the person of the waiter. In practical terms Ayckbourn uses him very much as an orchestral conductor. Not only does the waiter dictate the pace of the play, but he also, through his movement from table to table, brings out the relevant items of conversation which inform us of the personalities and activities of the diners.

In his original conception Alan Ayckbourn had intended that the waiter from *Drinking Companion* should continue through into *Between Mouthfuls* to give a balance to the male characters within all five plays. In this piece he is the central pivot around which the play revolves and is faced with a most difficult task. He should remain very much part of the furniture. Self-effacing, long-suffering and yet ever attentive. His timing must be impeccable yet unobtrusive. He must resist the temptation to steal the limelight. A performance which could earn him a nomination to be the fourth Marx Brother would destroy the fine balance of the play. We are to be told the story of the two couples and he is there to turn the pages. I have seen productions of this piece where the waiter has been a walking disaster-area-cum-cabaret-act with the Pearces and the Chalmers's in support roles. This is certainly not what Alan Ayckbourn intended and can destroy the play. There is certainly high comedy here within the writing and the set pieces of business provided by the author. They stand up for themselves and do not require the services of a bufoon to enliven them.

The play opens simply enough. The waiter is polite and patient in the face of Mr Pearce's rather high-handed attitude. His treatment of Mrs Pearce is exactly the same despite her irritability. One can almost see 'The customer is always right' branded on his forehead as he hovers solicitously around their table. By this time we have obtained a pretty clear picture of the Pearces and as the waiter moves away, their voices fade out.

As an audience we are ready to accept this piece of stylisation. We are only going to hear what the waiter hears and like the surreptitious keyhole-peeper we are longing for more.

When Polly and Martin Chalmers enter we detect that all is not well. Polly seems a little too adamant in her refusal to eat in the same restaurant as the Pearces or be forced to join their table. There is an edginess between them which as yet remains unexplained. And before we are enlightened any further the waiter moves away.

So the play continues. It is rather like a huge jig-saw: as each piece fits into place our appetites are whetted and our attention is ensured to the bitter end.

The Pearces go on bickering, while Polly tries desperately to encourage Martin to take notice of her. Gradually we learn of the foreign holidays and of Pearce's infidelities. Both conversations become more animated as the waiter moves swiftly between the tables. He must remain a calm contrast to what is going on around him. His movement must be uncluttered and economical so that both the conversations and his interjections flow smoothly from one into the other. During the fierce exchange between Pearce and his wife his cool detached manner heightens their argument and places the comedy onto a high level. He performs the same function when Polly confesses her guilt but here our reactions are tinged with sympathy. The fact that Martin is more concerned about his job prospects than his wife's unfaithfulness brings us firmly down on Polly's side as she storms out.

The rather predictable ending to the play with the waiter still performing his subservient duties leaves us with rather a nasty taste in our mouths.

This is comedy situation writing at its best. Its pitfalls are many and the play must be carefully handled. It has to be a team effort with all five actors responding with great sympathy and understanding to each other. Hours must be spent on the timing of both lines and business in order that it appears effortless in performance. There is no necessity to force the laughter from an audience since smooth, confident playing will bring its own rewards.

Gosforth's Fête

This play takes the comedy a stage further. Once again there are the stock characters. The almost left-on-the-shelf schoolmistress, the enthusiastic young cub-master complete with pole, woggle and shorts as well as a bumbling, incompetent vicar. Added to these are a human tornado, a picture-hatted, true-blue lady councillor, a rampaging cub pack, a waterlogged tea-tent and the vagaries of the English weather: with these ingredients it is easy to predict what the outcome is likely to be.

We are not to be disappointed. The scene is beautifully set in the opening dialogue between Emma Pearce and Milly. Obviously Donald Pearce has cried off at the last minute and offered some feeble excuse. Everything is 'a bit behindhand', and the Second Little Pendon Pack have already begun to indulge in most un-cub-like activities. What is more the weather 'looks a little threatening'. We have just absorbed this information when Gosforth himself bursts onto the scene as if 'in the thick of battle'.

He is like a whirlwind. He is supporting the entire weight of the garden party on his shoulders. Despite having delegated various areas of responsibility, it is clear that he would have preferred to do everything himself. He does not suffer fools gladly, bristles with self-importance and hardly ever listens to anyone else's point of view. His speech when he describes the afternoon's activities to the bewildered Mrs. Pearce gives him a wonderful opportunity to impress with his knowledge, organisational ability and merry quips. As a character we feel we have almost had enough of him already. However he is to plough mercilessly on giving us important information about the amplifier and summarily dismissing the local doctor's contribution to the event.

Just as we have almost reached screaming point the Rev. John Braithwaite comes in to offer us light relief. His disorganisation in the face of the aggressive regimentation of Gosforth becomes a virtue and we take him to our hearts. Unlike Gordon *he* is a listener. His problem seems to be that he never really takes anything in since the effort of lending a sympathetic ear appears to be totally exhausting.

We have reached a lull in the proceedings which takes us gently into the startling revelations of Milly's pregnancy and Gosforth's unsympathetic reactions. Once the microphone has been dropped and it is obvious to the audience that the conversation is being broadcast, the pace must pick up again in preparation for Stewart's explosive entrance.

The sight of this earnest, very red-faced young man in full scouting regalia shouting swear words at the top of his voice is one of the first visual triumphs of the play. He is completely beside himself and must play the scene for all it is worth until his collapse into the chair as he mutters incredulously 'Four acres. Four acres...'. The rain begins to hammer down and Stewart, indulging in unfamiliar alcohol, gets progressively more tipsy. Hometruths are exchanged between Milly and her rather dull fiance and even the vicar gets in on the act adding more fuel to the fire.

With the entrance of Gosforth carrying the tea urn the activity begins to forge ahead yet again. The pace of the play quickens as we approach its climax. Mrs. Pearce arrives bespattered with mud as a result of misdirection by the cubs. Gosforth begins his speech of welcome as the vicar succeeds in jamming the tap on the tea urn. The frantic attempts to stem the flow of liquid with innumerable plastic cups is punctuated with the strains of well-known camp-fire songs rendered by the drunken Stewart. Mrs. Pearce's Party Political Broadcast is lost during the ensuing melee and her reward is electrocution. Once again the vicar manages to involve himself in these shocking events. All hell is let loose. Gosforth's final, desperate endeavours to bring order out of chaos end in his being catapulted out of the tent into the pouring rain and churned up mud as Stewart's home-made podium collapses around him. Fitting retribution indeed for his misdemeanour with the hapless Milly.

This is English farce at its best. It combines hilarious visual images with frenzied dialogue. The secret is to keep everything going once it is launched. The synchronization of dialogue and action is paramount and needs careful rehearsal. Everything in this final section builds to the electrocution of Emma and must be pointed in that direction. It must be plotted cold-bloodedly so that the laughter from the audience is controlled and built to a crescendo at the right moment. Even then it must be kept bubbling along to rise once more as Gosforth pitches out of the tent entrance.

As with *Between Mouthfuls* the playing has to be precise and

uncluttered. Even though so much is going on the audience must
not miss a trick. The successful acting of farce calls for great
discipline on stage, for ensemble playing of a very high order and
a well-developed dexterity in handling stage properties. If it is
successful it should leave the audience not only with sore ribs but
also gasping in admiration. The potential for this is certainly
present in the final stages of *Gosforth's Fete*. It is, technically, the
most difficult section of the five-play collection. By now the
audience is ready for a break. A gradual wind-down is called for
and this is provided in the gentle finale to *Confusions*.

A Talk in the Park

This short, revue-type piece of writing is seen by Alan Ayckbourn
as a curtain call for the five actors. It is a way of saying goodnight
and at the same time underlining the basic themes of lonliness
and misunderstanding which have caused so much confusion in
what has gone before.

As a direct contrast to what we have seen earlier this piece does
not use any tricks but relies almost entirely on the dialogue for its
effect. It is a picture of desolation designed to focus our attention
keenly on the plight of the protagonists. They give vent to their
innermost feelings. The audience takes on the role of confessor
since no-one in the play seems prepared to listen. We are aware that
some form of human chess is being played in front of us which we
are powerless to control. Thus it is that the characters' frustrations
become our frustrations. They impress themselves upon us more
strongly because of the simplicity of the presentation.

Arthur is desperate for companionship. Talking to himself has
lost its appeal. His inconsequential chat about his collection of
people and cigarette cards demonstrates the quality of his
loneliness. The inanimate objects are real; his human aquisitions
imaginary. They have been ships that pass in the night making only
a superficial impression on him. He chooses women to talk to
because he feels they will listen. He cannot cope in a man's world
and is desperately trying to recapture his childhood security.
However Beryl is the wrong woman to choose. She has had her
share of companionship which has turned sour and she abruptly
leaves to unburden herself on the respectable looking Charles.

Beryl's problem is that whenever she seeks advice she never
listens. Her mind is already made up. The obvious solution is
starting her in the face. However she is so utterly besotted by the
man who continually ill-treats her that she is unable to stand back

and view the situation rationally. Hers is a self-enforced loneliness. She lacks the courage to act positively and yet tortures herself with an analysis of the situation out of which she may never escape. She simply needs to get it off her chest before returning to do battle once more. It is almost as if she is seeking absolution. The venom and air of self-destruction in her speech sends Charles running for cover.

Despite his apparent affluence he too is a sad figure. A born pessimist who is content to blame fate and the world in general for all his trials and tribulations. After the death of his wife, 'woodworm' has eaten into his life. He has given up trying. His business is shaky and, despite his protestations that he doesn't 'go around boring people' with his problems, this seems to be the only way left in which he can express himself. Disaster is inevitable and non-one will persuade him otherwise. He too has lost his ability to cope. If we are to believe what he says about his life five years ago then this acceptance of impending doom and the degeneration of middle age make his situation even more pathetic.

Doreen's predicament is that, basically, she cannot stand men. The masculine image which they propagate is too much for her and deep down inside, while she is still fascinated, she has tried to reject them. She is now pouring out her 'affection' and reason for living on to her dog. Her obsession has taken over and her puppy has become her substitute male companion. However she has just taken him to the vet to be neutered. When she tells him of his visit 'his little ears prick up and his tails wags'. She has at last got her own back. She is now the dominant one and can make all the decisions. Her inadequacy in the normal world and her unhealthy preoccupation with the male species naturally causes Ernest to flee for his life.

This young man refuses to accept his responsibilities. On the surface he is self-assured and 'one of the boys'. However his superficial attitude to everything around him has created a rift in his marriage which is obviously going to widen as the years go by. He is much happier to 'cut and run' rather than face his problems and try to do something about them. To some extent we sympathize with his feelings of emasculation yet censure his lack of positive action. His retreat from the noise of 'the man-made world' is an act of cowardice.

As an audience we sit and listen as the words come pouring out and in doing so are reminded of our own failings. How often have we ignored those around us because we are too busy running our own lives? We become blinkered to the needs of others as we retreat deeper into our own concerns.

The concluding round of pleading followed by the acceptance of rejection and the final line 'might as well talk to yourself' says it all. The curtain comes down leaving us somewhat disconcerted in our seats.

As already stated Alan Ayckbourn is a self-confessed commercial playwright. He has probably reached a wider public than any other author in the last fifty years.

In *Confusions* we are faced with a small-scale sweep of his capabilities. His craftsmanship is not in dispute. He is equally at home with comedy of character and high farce. He can make us roar with laughter and move us to tears. Above all he is, as Arthur says in *A Talk in the Park* a 'collector of people'.

For our part we must look deeper into his work. His beautifully wrapped packages contain hidden messages for us all. It is usually after the plays are over that we begin to question our motives as we recognise the seriousness of the subject matter.

It is in this way that the memory of an Ayckbourn play remains with members of his audiences for a long time and brings us back over and over again. It is not just the laughter which is remembered but the human collisions that we have witnessed, which possess the power to awaken our compassion. At one of his plays we are 'taken out of ourselves' in the real 'theatrical' meaning of that phrase, which surely is a total vindication of Alan Ayckbourn's achievements as Britain's most popular playwright.

Suggestions for further reading

Ayckbourn's own plays

The following collections are available in Penguin paperbacks:

Joking Apart and other plays, also containing *Ten Times Table, Just Between Ourselves* and *Sisterly Feelings,*

The Norman Conquests, comprising *Table Manners, Living Together* and *Round and Round the Garden.*

Three Plays, containing *Absurd Person Singular, Absent Friends* and *Bedroom Farce.*

Most of the other full-length plays are available in acting editions from Samuel French Ltd.

Books

Elsom, John,. *Post-War British Theatre* (London Routledge and Kegan Paul, 1976).

Hayman, Ronald, *British Theatre since 1955* (London: Oxford University Press, 1979).

Kerensky, Oleg, *The New British Drama* (London: Hamish Hamilton, 1977).

Taylor, John Russell, *The Second Wave* (London Methuen, 1971).

Watson, Ian, *Conversations with Ayckbourn* (London: Macdonald Futura, 1981)

Interviews and features

Billington Michael, 'Ayckbourn is a Left-Wing Writer Using a Right-Wing Form . . .', *The Guardian,* 14 August 1974.

Connell, Brian, 'Times Profile', *The Times,* 5 January 1976.

Coveney, Michael, Interview, *Plays and Players,* September 1975.

Cowley, Deborah, 'Alan Ayckbourn's Theatre Conquests', *Reader's Digest,* November 1979.

Hayman, Ronald, *The Times,* 4 July 1973.

Heilpern, John, 'Striking Sparks off Suburbia', *The Observer,* 13 February 1977.

Miller, Russell, 'The Hit-Man from Scarborough'. *The Sunday Times Colour Magazine,* 20 February 1977.

Naipaul, Shiva, 'Scarborough – Where to Succeed in Show Business', *Radio Times*, 22 August 1975.

New York Times interview: 'Mr Ayckbourn, is Sex Funny? Depends. With Me, it's Hilarious', 20 October 1974.

Oakes, Philip, 'Lines and Deadlines', *The Sunday Times*, 3 June 1973.

Page, Malcolm, 'The Serious Side of Alan Ayckbourn', *Modern Drama*, March 1983.

Spurling, Hilary, 'Side by Side in Scarborough', *TLS*, 13 February 1981.

Taylor, John Russell, 'British Dramatists: the New Arrivals, No. 9'. *Plays and Players*, December 1970.

Thornber, Robin, 'A Farceur, Relatively Speaking', *The Guardian*, 7 August 1970.

Tinker, Jack, *Daily Mail*, 28 February 1978.

Wale, Michael, *The Financial Times*, 8 July 1971.

Watson, Ian, 'Ayckbourn of Scarborough', *Municipal Entertainment*, May 1978.

Watts, Janet, *The Observer*, 4 March 1979.

Reviews of 'Confusions'

Billington, Michael – *Guardian*, 20 May 1976.

Wordle, Erving – *The Times*, 20 May 1976.

Young, B.A. – *Financial Times*, 20 May 1976.

Mother Figure: Lucy and Terry

Mother Figure: Lucy and Rosemary

Gosforth's Fête: Milly and Mrs Pearce

Gosforth's Fête: Stewart and Vicar

A Talk in the Park: Doreen and Ernest *(above)*; Arthur and Beryl *(below)*

CONFUSIONS

Gosforth's Fête: Stewart

CONFUSIONS

First presented by Michael Codron at the Apollo
Theatre, London, on May 19th, 1976, with the following
cast of characters:

MOTHER FIGURE

Lucy	Pauline Collins
Rosemary	Sheila Gish
Terry	Derek Fowlds

DRINKING COMPANION

Harry	John Alderton
Paula	Pauline Collins
Bernice	Sheila Gish
Waiter	James Cossins

BETWEEN MOUTHFULS

Waiter	John Alderton
Pearce	James Cossins
Mrs Pearce	Sheila Gish
Martin	Derek Fowlds
Polly	Pauline Collins

GOSFORTH'S FÊTE

Mrs Pearce	Sheila Gish
Milly	Pauline Collins
Gosforth	John Alderton
Vicar	James Cossins
Stewart	Derek Fowlds

A TALK IN THE PARK

Arthur	John Alderton
Beryl	Pauline Collins
Charles	James Cossins
Doreen	Sheila Gish
Ernest	Derek Fowlds

The Plays directed by Alan Strachan
Settings by Alan Tagg

The action takes place in a living-room, a bar, a restaurant, a marquee and a park

Time—the present

AUTHOR'S NOTE

These plays, although loosely linked, can of course be performed individually. When played together, it is recommended that they be presented in the order in which they appear here.

The entertainment was written originally for a cast of five (three male, two female). Obviously there are a variety of casting combinations which can be employed, depending on the actors available.

MOTHER FIGURE

Lucy's sitting-room

It is a suburban room, fairly untidy, with evidence of small children. There are two doors—one to the kitchen and back door, one to the bedrooms and front door

Lucy hurries in from the bedrooms on her way to the kitchen. She is untidy, unmade-up, in dressing-gown and slippers

Lucy (*calling behind her*) Nicholas! Stay in your own bed and leave Sarah alone.

The telephone rings

Lucy goes out to the kitchen, returning at once with a glass of water

All right, Jamie, darling. Mummy's coming with a dinkie . . . (*As she passes the telephone, she lifts the receiver off the rest and almost immediately replaces it*) Mummy's coming, Jamie, Mummy's coming.

Lucy goes off to the bedroom with the glass

The front door chimes sound. A pause, then they sound again

Lucy returns from the bedrooms

Sarah! You're a naughty, naughty girl. I told you not to play with Jamie's syrup. That's for Jamie's toothipegs . . .

The door chimes sound again

Lucy ignores these and goes off to the kitchen. She returns almost at once with a toilet roll, hauling off handfuls of it as she goes to perform some giant mopping-up operation

Nicholas, if you're not in your bed by the time I come up, I shall smack your botty.

There are two rings on the back door bell

Lucy goes off to the bedroom

A pause

Rosemary, a rather frail, mousey-looking woman, comes in from the kitchen

Rosemary (*calling timidly*) Woo-hoo!

Lucy returns from the bedroom

Lucy (*calling as before*) Now go to sleep. At once. (*Seeing Rosemary*) Oh.
Rosemary Hallo. I thought you must be in.
Lucy (*puzzled*) Hallo?
Rosemary I thought you were in.
Lucy Yes.
Rosemary You are.
Lucy Yes.
Rosemary Hallo.
Lucy Hallo. (*A slight pause*) Who are you?
Rosemary Next door.
Lucy What?
Rosemary From next door. Mrs Oates. Rosemary. Do you remember?
Lucy (*vaguely*) Oh, yes. Hallo.
Rosemary Hallo. I did ring both bells but nobody seemed . . .
Lucy No. I don't take much notice of bells.
Rosemary Oh.
Lucy I've rather got my hands full.
Rosemary Oh yes. With the children, you mean? How are they?
Lucy Fine.
Rosemary All well?
Lucy Yes.
Rosemary Good. It's three you've got, isn't it?
Lucy Yes.
Rosemary Still, I expect it's time well spent.
Lucy I haven't much option.
Rosemary No.
Lucy Well.
Rosemary Oh, don't let me—if you want to get on . . .
Lucy No.
Rosemary I mean, if you were going to bed.
Lucy Bed?
Rosemary (*indicating Lucy's attire*) Well . . .
Lucy Oh, no. I didn't get dressed today, that's all.
Rosemary Oh. Not ill?
Lucy No.
Rosemary Oh.
Lucy I just wasn't going anywhere.
Rosemary Oh, well . . .
Lucy I haven't been anywhere for weeks.
Rosemary That's a shame.
Lucy I don't think I've got dressed for weeks, either.

Rosemary Ah. No, well, I must say we haven't seen you. Not that we've been looking but we haven't seen you.

Lucy No. Do you want to sit down?

Rosemary Oh, thank you. Just for a minute.

Lucy If you can find somewhere. (*She moves the odd toy*)

Rosemary (*sitting*) Yes, we were wondering if you were alright, actually. My husband and I—Terry, that's my husband—he was remarking that we hadn't seen you for a bit.

Lucy No.

Rosemary We heard the children, of course. Not to complain of, mind you, but we heard them but we didn't see you.

Lucy No. (*She picks up various toys during the following and puts them in the play-pen*)

Rosemary Or your husband.

Lucy No.

Rosemary But then I said to Terry, if they need us they've only to ask. They know where we are. If they want to keep themselves to themselves, that's all right by us. I mean, that's why they put up that great big fence so they could keep themselves to themselves. And that's all right by us.

Lucy Good.

Rosemary And then ten minutes ago, we got this phone call.

Lucy Phone call?

Rosemary Yes. Terry answered it—that's my husband—and they say will you accept a transfer charge call from a public phone box in Middlesbrough and Terry says, hallo, that's funny, he says, who do we know in Middlesbrough and I said, not a soul and he says, well, that's funny, Terry says, well who is it? How do we know we know him? If we don't know him, we don't want to waste money talking to him but if we do, it might be an emergency and we won't sleep a wink. And the operator says, well suit yourself, take it or leave it, it's all the same to me. So we took it and it was your husband.

Lucy Harry?

Rosemary Harry, yes. Mr Compton.

Lucy What did he want?

Rosemary Well—you. He was worried. He's been ringing you for days. He's had the line checked but there's been no reply.

Lucy Oh.

Rosemary Has it not been ringing?

Lucy Possibly. I don't take much notice of bells. (*She goes to listen for the children*)

Rosemary Oh. Anyway, he sounded very worried. So I said I'd pop round and make sure. I took his number in case you wanted to . . .

Lucy is clearly not listening

Are you all right?

Lucy Yes, I was listening for Nicholas.

Rosemary Oh. That's the baby?

Lucy No.

Rosemary (*warmly*) Ah.

Lucy I'm sorry. I'm being very rude. It's just I haven't—spoken to anyone for days. My husband isn't home much.

Rosemary Oh, I quite understand. Would you like his number?

Lucy What?

Rosemary Your husband's telephone number in Middlesbrough. Would you like it? He said he'd hang on. It's from a hotel.

Lucy No.

Rosemary Oh.

Lucy Whatever he has to say to me, he can say to my face or not at all.

Rosemary Ah. (*Laying a slip of paper gingerly on the coffee-table*) Well, it's there.

Lucy Would you care for a drink or something?

Rosemary A drink? Oh—well—what's the time? Well—I don't know if I should. Half past—oh yes, well—why not? Yes, please. Why not? A little one.

Lucy Orange or lemon?

Rosemary I beg your pardon?

Lucy Orange juice or lemon juice? Or you can have milk.

Rosemary Oh, I see. I thought you meant . . .

Lucy Come on. Orange or lemon? I'm waiting.

Rosemary Is there a possibility of some coffee?

Lucy No.

Rosemary Oh.

Lucy It'll keep you awake. I'll get you an orange, it's better for you.

Rosemary Oh . . .

Lucy (*as she goes*) Sit still. Don't run around. I won't be a minute.

Lucy goes out into the kitchen

Rosemary sits nervously. She rises after a second, looks guiltily towards the kitchen and sits again. The door chimes sound. Rosemary looks towards the kitchen. There is no sign of Lucy. The door chimes sound again. Rosemary gets up hesitantly

Rosemary (*calling*) Mrs—er . . .

Lucy (*off, in the kitchen*) Wait, wait, wait! I'm coming . . .

The door chimes sound again

Rosemary runs off to the front door. Lucy returns from the kitchen with a glass of orange juice

Here we are, Rosemary, I . . . (*She looks round the empty room, annoyed. Calling*) Rosemary! It's on the table.

Lucy puts the orange juice on the coffee-table and goes out to the kitchen again. Rosemary returns from the hall with Terry, a rather pudgy man in shirt sleeves

Rosemary (*sotto voce*) Come in a minute.

Terry I'm watching the telly.

Rosemary Just for a minute.

Terry I wondered where you'd got to. I mean, all you had to do was give her the number . . .

Rosemary I want you to meet her. See what you think. I don't think she's well.

Terry How do you mean?

Rosemary She just seems . . .

Terry Is she ill?

Rosemary I don't know . . .

Terry Well, either she's ill or she isn't.

Rosemary Ssh.

Lucy returns from the kitchen with a plate of biscuits

Lucy Here we are now. (*Seeing Terry*) Oh.

Terry Evening.

Lucy Hallo.

Rosemary My husband.

Lucy Terry, isn't it?

Terry Yes.

Lucy That's a nice name, isn't it? (*Pointing to the sofa*) Sit down there then. Have you got your orange juice, Rosemary?

Terry sits

Rosemary Yes, thank you. (*She picks up the glass of orange juice and sits*)

Terry Orange juice?

Rosemary Yes.

Terry What are you doing drinking that?

Rosemary I like orange juice.

Lucy Now, here's some very special choccy bics but you mustn't eat them all. I'm going to trust you. (*She starts tidying up again*)

Rosemary (*still humouring her*) Lovely. (*She mouths "say something" to Terry*)

Terry Yes. Well, how are you keeping then—er, sorry, I'm forgetting. Lesley, isn't it?

Lucy Mrs Compton.

Terry Yes. Mrs Compton. How are you?

Lucy I'm very well, thank you, Terry. Nice of you to ask.

Terry And what about Har—Mr Compton?

Lucy Very well. When I last saw him. Rosemary dear, try not to make all that noise when you drink.

Rosemary Sorry.

Terry Yes, we were saying that your husband's job obviously takes him round and about a lot.

Lucy Yes. (*She starts folding nappies*)

Terry Doesn't get home as much as he'd like, I expect.

Lucy I've no idea.

Terry But then it takes all sorts. Take me, I'm home on the nose six o'clock every night. That's the way she wants it. Who am I . . .? (*Pause*) Yes, I think I could quite envy your husband, sometimes. Getting about a bit. I mean, when you think about it, it's more natural. For a man. His natural way of life. Right back to the primitive. Woman stays in the cave, man the hunter goes off roving at will. Mind you, I think the idea originally was he went off hunting for food. Different sort of game these days, eh?

Rosemary (*hissing*) Terry!

Terry Be after something quite different these days, eh? (*He nods and winks*)

Lucy Now don't get silly, Terry.

Terry What? Ah—beg your pardon.

A pause. Terry munches a biscuit. Rosemary sips her orange juice

Rosemary Very pleasant orange juice.

Lucy Full of vitamin C.

Terry No, I didn't want to give you the wrong impression there. But seriously, I was saying to Rosie here, you can't put a man in a cage. You try to do that, you've lost him. See my point?

Lucy That can apply to women, too, surely?

Rosemary Yes, quite right.

Terry What do you mean, quite right?

Rosemary Well . . .

Terry You're happy enough at home, aren't you?

Rosemary Yes, but—yes—but . . .

Terry Well then, that's what I'm saying. You're the woman, you're happy enough at home looking after that. I'm the man, I have to be out and about.

Rosemary I don't know about that. You'd never go out at all unless I pushed you.

Terry What do you mean? I'm out all day.

Rosemary Only because you have to be. You wouldn't be if you didn't have to be. When you don't, you come in, sit down, watch the television and go to bed.

Terry I have to relax.

Rosemary You're always relaxing.

Terry Don't deny me relaxing.

Rosemary I don't.

Terry Yes, you do, you just said . . .

Lucy Now, don't quarrel. I won't have any quarrelling.

Terry Eh?

Rosemary Sorry.

Lucy Would you like an orange drink as well, Terry? Is that what it is?

Terry Er . . . Oh no—I don't go in for that sort of drink much, if you know what I mean. (*He winks, then reaches for a biscuit*) I'll have another one of these though, if you don't mind?

Lucy Just a minute, how many have you had?

Terry This is my second. It's only my second.

Lucy Well, that's all. No more after that. I'll get you some milk. You better have something that's good for you.

Terry (*half rising*) Oh no—thank you, not milk, no.

Lucy (*going to the kitchen*) Wait there. (*Seeing Terry has half risen*) And don't jump about while you're eating, Terry.

Lucy goes out to the kitchen

Terry You're right. She's odd.

Rosemary I said she was.

Terry No wonder he's gone off.

Rosemary Perhaps that's why she's odd.

Terry Why?

Rosemary Because he's gone off.

Terry Rubbish. And we'll have less of that, too, if you don't mind.

Rosemary What?

Terry All this business about me never going out of the house.

Rosemary It's true.

Terry It's not true and it makes me out to be some bloody idle loafer.

Rosemary All I said . . .

Terry And even if it is true, you have no business saying it in front of other people.

Rosemary Oh, honestly, Terry, you're so touchy. I can't say a thing right these days, can I?

Terry Very little. Now you come to mention it.

Rosemary Niggle, niggle, niggle. You keep on at me the whole time. I'm frightened to open my mouth these days. I don't know what's got into you lately. You're in a filthy mood from the moment you get up till you go to bed . . .

Terry What are you talking about?

Rosemary Grumbling and moaning . . .

Terry Oh, shut up.

Rosemary You're a misery to live with these days, you really are.

Terry I said, shut up.

Rosemary (*more quietly*) I wish to God you'd go off somewhere sometimes, I really do.

Terry Don't tempt me. I bloody feel like it occasionally, I can tell you.

Rosemary (*tearfully*) Oh, lovely . . .

Terry If you think I enjoy spending night after night sitting looking at you . . . (*He throws the biscuit down*) What am I eating these damn things for . . . you're mistaken. (*Thirsty from the biscuits, he grabs her orange juice glass and drains it in one*)

Rosemary That's mine, do you mind. (*She rises and stamps her foot*)

Terry Come on. Let's go. (*He jumps up*)

Rosemary That was my orange juice when you've quite finished.

Lucy enters with a glass of milk

Lucy Now what are you doing jumping about?

Rosemary sits

Terry We've got to be going, I'm sorry.

Lucy Not till you've finished. Sit down.

Terry Listen, I'm sorry we . . .

Lucy (*seeing Rosemary's distraught state*) What's the matter with Rosemary?

Rosemary (*sniffing*) Nothing . . .

Terry Nothing.

Lucy What have you been doing to her?

Terry Nothing.

Lucy Here's your milk.

Terry Thank you.

Lucy You don't deserve it.

Terry I don't want it.

Lucy Don't be tiresome.

Terry I hate the damned stuff.

Lucy I'm not going to waste my breath arguing with you, Terry. It's entirely up to you if you don't want to be big and strong.

Terry Now, look . . .

Lucy If you want to be a little weakling, that's up to you. Just don't come whining to me when all your nails and teeth fall out. Now then, Rosemary, let's see to you. (*She puts down the milk and picks up the biscuits*) Would you like a choccy biccy?

Rosemary No, thank you.

Lucy Come on, they're lovely choccy, look. Milk choccy . . .

Rosemary No, honestly.

Terry Rosie, are you coming or not?

Lucy Well, have a drink, then. Blow your nose and have a drink, that's a good girl. (*Seeing the glass*) Oh, it's all gone. You've drunk that quickly, haven't you?

Rosemary I didn't drink it. He did.

Lucy What?

Rosemary He drank it.

Lucy Terry, did you drink her orange juice?

Terry Look, there's a programme I want to watch . . .

Lucy Did you drink Rosemary's orange juice?

Terry Look, good night . . .

Rosemary Yes, he did.

Lucy Well, I think that's really mean.

Rosemary He just takes anything he wants.

Lucy Really mean.

Rosemary Never thinks of asking.

Terry I'm going.

Lucy Not before you've apologized to Rosemary.

Terry Good night.

Terry goes out

Lucy (*calling after him*) And don't you dare come back until you're ready to apologize. (*To Rosemary*) Never mind him. Let him go. He'll be back.

Rosemary That's the way to talk to him.

Lucy What?

Rosemary That's the way he ought to be talked to more often.

Lucy I'm sorry. I won't have that sort of behaviour. Not from anyone.

Rosemary He'll sulk now. For days.

Lucy Well, let him. It doesn't worry us, does it?

Rosemary No. It's just sometimes—things get on top of you—and then he comes back at night—and he starts on at me and I . . . (*She cries*) Oh dear—I'm so sorry—I didn't mean to . . .

Lucy (*cooing*) Come on now. Come on . . .

Rosemary I've never done this. I'm sorry . . .

Lucy That's all right. There, there.

Rosemary I'm sorry. (*She continues to weep*)

Lucy Look who's watching you.

Rosemary Who?

Lucy (*picking up a doll*) Mr Poddle. Mr Poddle's watching you. (*She holds up the doll*) You don't want Mr Poddle to see you crying, do you? Do you?

Rosemary (*lamely*) No . . .

Lucy Do we, Mr Poddle? (*She shakes Mr Poddle's head*) No, he says, no. Stop crying, Rosie. (*She nods Mr Poddle's head*) Stop crying, Rosie. Yes—yes.

Rosemary gives an embarrassed giggle

That's better. Was that a little laugh, Mr Poddle? Was that a little laugh?

Lucy wiggles Mr Poddle about, bringing him close up to Rosemary's face and taking him away again

Was that a little laugh? Was that a little laugh? Was that a little laugh?

Rosemary giggles uncontrollably

Terry enters from the hall and stands amazed

Terry Er . . .

Lucy and Rosemary become aware of him

Er—I've locked myself out.

Lucy Have you come back to apologize?

Terry You got the key, Rosie?

Rosemary Yes.

Terry Let's have it then.

Lucy Not until you apologize.

Terry Look, I'm not apologizing to anyone. I just want the key. To get back into my own house, if you don't mind. Now, come on.

Rosemary (*producing the key from her bag*) Here.

Lucy Rosemary, don't you dare give it to him.

Terry Eh?

Rosemary What?

Lucy Not until he apologizes.

Terry Rosie, give me the key.

Lucy No, Rosemary. I'll take it. Give it to me.

Terry Rosie.

Lucy Rosemary.

Rosemary (*torn*) Er . . .

Lucy (*very fiercely*) Rosemary, will you give me that key at once.

Rosemary gives Lucy the key. Terry regards Lucy

Terry Would you mind most awfully giving me the key to my own front door?

Lucy Certainly.

Terry Thank you so much.

Lucy Just as soon as you've apologized to Rosemary.

Terry I've said, I'm not apologizing to anyone.

Lucy Then you're not having the key.

Terry Now listen, I've got a day's work to do tomorrow. I'm damned if I'm going to start playing games with some frustrated nutter . . .

Rosemary Terry . . .

Lucy Take no notice of him, Rosemary, he's just showing off.

Terry Are you going to give me that key or not?

Lucy Not until you apologize.

Terry All right. I'll have to come and take it off you, won't I?

Lucy You try. You just dare try, my boy.

Terry All right. (*He moves towards Lucy*)

Rosemary Terry . . .

Lucy Just you try and see what happens.

Terry (*halted by her tone; uncertainly*) I'm not joking.

Lucy Neither am I.

Terry Look, I don't want to . . . Just give me the key, there's a good . . .

Lucy Not until you apologize to Rosemary.

Terry Oh, for the love of . . . All right (*To Rosemary*) Sorry.

Lucy Say it nicely.

Terry I'm very sorry, Rosie. Now give us the key, for God's sake.

Lucy When you've drunk your milk. Sit down and drink your milk.

Terry Oh, blimey . . . (*He sits*)

Lucy That's better.

Terry I hate milk.

Lucy Drink it up.

Terry scowls and picks up the glass. Rosemary, unseen by Lucy, sticks her tongue out at him. Terry bangs down his glass and moves as if to hit her

    Terry!
Terry She stuck her tongue out at me.
Lucy Sit still.
Terry But she . . .
Lucy Sit!

Terry sits scowling. Rosemary smirks at him smugly

    (*Seeing her*) And don't do that, Rosemary. If the wind changes, you'll get stuck like it. And sit up straight and don't slouch.

Rosemary does so

Terry (*taking a sip of the milk*) This is horrible.

Silence. He takes another sip

    It's warm.

Silence. Another sip

Terry There's a football international on television, you know.
Lucy Not until you've drunk that up, there isn't. Come on, Rosemary. Help Terry to drink it. "Georgie Porgie Pudding and Pie, Kissed the girls and . . . ?"
Rosemary "Made them cry."
Lucy Good.
Rosemary ⎱ "When the boys came out to play, Georgie Porgie ⎰ (*Speaking
Lucy   ⎰ ran away."   ⎱ together*)
Terry (*finishing his glass with a giant swallow*) All gone. (*He wipes his mouth*)
Lucy Good boy.
Terry Can I have the key now, please?
Lucy Here you are.

Terry goes to take it

    What do you say?
Terry Thank you.
Lucy All right. Off you go, both of you.
Rosemary (*kissing her on the cheek*) Night night.
Lucy Night night, dear. Night night, Terry.
Terry (*kissing Lucy likewise*) Night night.
Lucy Sleep tight.
Terry Hope the bugs don't bite.
Lucy Hold Rosemary's hand, Terry.

Rosemary and Terry hold hands

    See her home safely.
Terry Night.

Rosemary Night.
Lucy Night night.

Terry and Rosemary go off hand in hand

Lucy blows kisses

(*With a sigh*) Blooming kids. Honestly.

The telephone rings. Lucy, as she passes it, picks it up and replaces it as before. As she does so, the Lights fade to a single spot in a call-box. Harry is there, with the receiver in his hand

Harry Oh, blast, not again. Hallo—hallo—oh, damn and blast. (*He jiggles the receiver*) Operator? Operator? Hallo—hallo . . . Operator, there must be a fault on this line. . . . The line I have been trying unsuccessfully to dial. . . . Yes—six-four-one-nine. I mean, this is quite unforgivable. This is the third time I have reported it and I am still quite unable to make contact with my wife. . . . Yes, well, thank you for your sympathy. Let's try a little action, shall we? Because I'm going to take this to the top. . . . Yes, top. . . . What? . . . No—T for Toffee, O for Orange. . . . Oh, forget it. (*He rings off*) Give me strength.

Harry moves out of the box. As he does so, the Lights come up to full, and the set has now changed to—

DRINKING COMPANION

A three-star hotel bar

Discreet muzak is being played. Paula, a girl in her twenties, sits alone at a table, her coat and handbag beside her. On the table are her own vodka and tonic, and an unfinished whisky and soda. Harry, a man in his forties, returns and sits beside her

Harry Sorry. Sorry about that. Not getting lonely, are you?

Paula No.

Harry After all that, would you believe it, couldn't get through. I get the ringing tone then it just cuts off like that. I think there's a fault on the line. Cheers. (*He drinks*)

Paula Who were you trying to phone?

Harry (*evasively*) Oh, just—family. You know.

Paula Your wife?

Harry Yes . . .

Paula You're married?

Harry Yes.

Paula Have you got any children?

Harry Yes, yes . . . Can I get you another?

Paula Oh, well, just one more.

Harry (*calling*) Waiter. (*To Paula*) Same again, is it? Vodka and tonic?

Paula Lovely.

The Waiter appears

Harry Ah, Waiter. We want the same again, here, please. Vodka and tonic and scotch and soda.

Waiter Right, sir. (*He turns to go*)

Harry You'd better make them large ones.

Paula Oh, well . . .

Waiter Large whisky, large vodka, sir.

The Waiter goes

Harry You were saying you were just up here for a couple of days.

Paula That's right. We go back tomorrow.

Harry Extraordinary, you know. I was walking through Mason's this morning, on the ground floor, and I saw you two there, you and your friend—what's her name?

Paula Bernice.

Harry Bernice. Pretty name. Paula and Bernice—lovely names—and I thought to myself, hallo, they don't belong here. They look right out of place. Two lovely personalities like yours just don't go together with Mason's. No, I thought to myself—they're from London I wouldn't mind betting. Up for a visit. Promoting that—what was it you were selling?

Paula Perfume.

Harry And I said to myself, I wouldn't mind betting, Harry, that what's more those will be staying at the "Crown". And then it just so happens I look out of the door of the bar here and lo and behold—there you are, standing in the foyer.

Paula Coincidence.

Harry Not really. There's only one place to stay in this town. Well, you've got the "Wheatsheaf" or the "Black Horse" but they're not to be recommended, take it from me. When you're here, always plunk for the "Crown". How have your demonstrations been going? All right?

Paula Oh, extremely well. We're just on this short promotion tour for their new brand, you see.

Harry Is that the delicious fragrance I can smell even now?

Paula Oh yes, I think I've got some on.

Harry Very very nice. Very very nice indeed.

Paula It's proving very popular. It's exotic without being cloying and can be worn equally well day or night.

Harry You get commission on it, do you?

Paula Yes. They pay very well.

Harry Well, you need some inducement to come up here. What do you think of the place?

Paula It's all right, I suppose.

Harry Dreadful. Dead and alive place. Goes to bed at six o'clock at night, you know. No word of a lie. I've walked through the main street here, the main street mark you, at seven-thirty p.m. on a Saturday night and there has not been one single soul.

Paula Good gracious.

Harry Not one single soul. Empty. Deserted.

Paula You often here?

Harry Once every two months or so. Just a sales check really. I mean, my firm doesn't treat this area very seriously. Consumer demand is negligible. Our only stockist is Mason's. We're fairly exclusive, you see. That's why I was in there today going over our sales with Mr Molyneux. He's their chief chap, you know. Not at all bad when you get to know him but I must say our sales were very disappointing.

Paula We sold a lot of perfume.

Harry Yes, well, you'd be alright with that. But our line, you see, well, I suppose you'd call us *haute couture*—high fashion anyway. Cut above the average. Not much call for it up here. Predominantly working class, you see. Very small market.

The muzak fades out

Paula There's not many young people. We noticed that.

Harry No. There's not many girls, like, well, like yourself for instance. Now, you'd look very good in some of our stuff. Very good indeed.
Paula Really?
Harry Yes. (*Staring at her*) Orange. Tangerine shades. That's your colour.
Paula Is it?
Harry Definitely. You ought to go in for tangerine shades, take my tip. I'm good at that, you know. I can match a woman to her colour like that. Almost do it automatically these days.
Paula Really?
Harry You're what I call a modern girl, you see. You need modern shades, modern styling. Have you ever modelled by any chance?
Paula No, I don't think I've quite the . . .
Harry Oh, come on, come on. We don't always want them like sticks of celery, you know. Bit of shape never did a girl any harm. Some of our styles would really suit you.

The Waiter returns with the drinks

Ah. Thank you. Vodka and tonic there.
Waiter Thank you, sir. Thank you, madam.
Harry Could you charge it to Room two-four-nine, please?
Waiter Two-four-nine. Very good, sir. (*He waits*)
Harry Oh, just a second, just a second. (*Fumbling in his pocket and producing a handful of silver*) Here.
Waiter Oh. That's very good of you, sir, thank you.

The Waiter leaves

Harry Cheers. No, put it this way. In my particular line I've got to be able to look at a woman and say yes, you'd look good in so and so. Straightaway.
Paula Yes, I can see that.
Harry The same with you. No difference. Straightaway.
Paula Yes.

A slight pause

Harry You married, by any chance?
Paula No. Not likely.
Harry What, don't you fancy it?
Paula Not at the moment.
Harry Very sensible. Take my word. Steer clear.
Paula Don't let your wife hear you say that.
Harry Well, you know what I mean. Always envy what you haven't got, don't you?
Paula Oh yes?
Harry Freedom. I miss that. In the old days if I'd walked in here, say, and I'd met someone attractive—like I'm meeting you for instance . . .
Paula (*laughing*) Me?

Harry No—joking apart—seriously—well, you know, you could just allow things to happen.

Paula What sort of things?

Harry Well, that depends on the girl, doesn't it?

Paula Oh, I see.

Harry Cheers. Got a boyfriend, have you?

Paula One or two.

Harry Bet you have.

Paula Nothing serious. Nobody special.

Harry Playing the field?

Paula More or less.

Harry Why not? At your age. What are you? Twenty-one, I'd say at a guess.

Paula Some hope.

Harry What, younger than that?

Paula Twenty-five.

Harry Twenty-five? Get on with you. Thirty-seven.

Paula Oh yes?

Harry Thirty-seven. I don't look thirty-seven, do I?

Paula No.

Harry Not bad for thirty-seven. Ready for another one?

Paula No. I've hardly started this.

Harry No, in my opinion you young people today are doing the most sensible thing you can do. I mean, I know there's a lot of people of my generation that you could call narrow minded but I think it's just marvellous that a girl like you today, she can take her time, look around, get to know a few men for herself—you know, even sleep with them if she feels like it—and no hang-ups. Marvellous.

Paula What makes you think I do that?

Harry No, what I'm saying is . . .

Paula I don't go sleeping around, you know.

Harry No, that's not what I was saying. What I was saying . . .

Paula I don't fancy doing that.

Harry No, no, quite. But if you did happen to fancy it, there'd be nothing to stop you. That's what I was saying.

Paula Possibly.

Harry I mean, that's all I was saying. Cheers.

Paula Where do you live, then?

Harry Me? London. Well, just outside. Luton really.

Paula Oh.

Harry And you?

Paula Shepherd's Bush.

Harry Oh, really? I know Shepherd's Bush very well. Very pleasant. Parts of it.

Paula Yes, it is.

Pause

Harry No, to get back to our previous conversation. Look at it this way.

We're two adult people. This is now, the present, today. We can sit here and talk about—well, whatever we care to talk about—let's say for the sake of argument—sex—without feeling embarrassed. Now I think that's a tremendous step forward. When you think of the past.

Pause

I mean, I'm able to sit here, enjoy a drink in the middle of a public hotel, talking to a very, very attractive girl, if I may say so, and not feel in the least embarrassed. And she can do the same. You can do the same.

Paula It's a nice hotel.

Harry Not bad. Not marvellous, but not bad. Cheers.

Pause

The bedrooms are good. Have you got a nice room?

Paula Fine.

Harry Single?

Paula No. We've got a twin.

Harry We?

Paula Me and Bernice.

Harry Oh yes. That's your friend?

Paula Yes.

Harry I've got a double. I mean, it's just me in there but I've got a double. I can't bear small rooms, you see. Well, the firm's paying so why not. Besides, better to be prepared, isn't it?

Paula How do you mean?

Harry (*laughing*) No, it's a particularly nice room, two-four-nine. Always try and book it when I'm here. *En suite* bathroom, all the trimmings. Here, look—(*he produces his room key*)—two-four-nine, you see. Room two-four-nine. If you should come back here again, take my tip, try and get two-four-nine. I think it is the quietest room they've got. Not round the front, you see, it's round the side.

Paula That's good.

Harry Where are you two, then?

Paula Eh?

Harry What number?

Paula Oh, do you know, I can't remember offhand.

Harry Well, I hope your friend does. Otherwise you'll be wandering round all night, won't you? Probably finish up in two-four-nine if I'm lucky. (*He laughs*) Cheers.

Pause

Tell you what, are you likely to be paying a return visit any time?

Paula What, up here?

Harry Yes, you'll probably be coming back sometime, won't you?

Paula Shouldn't think so.

Harry You never know. When they see how much perfume you've sold, they'll probably send you straight back here to sell some more.

Paula It's only a temporary job.

Harry Well, if they should by any chance, you're bound to want to stay here again, aren't you? Nowhere else.

Paula I shouldn't think we'll . . .

Harry Well, what I was going to say is, would you like to have a quick look at two-four-nine? See if it'd suit you. You know, just in case you do come back.

Paula Oh no.

Harry No, I mean just literally pop upstairs, stick your nose round the door, see what you think.

Paula No, I couldn't really . . .

Harry Hang on, hang on, even better. Do you know what I've got up there? I've just remembered, I've got a bottle of whisky. Do you like whisky?

Paula No, I hate it.

Harry Of course, what am I saying, you're a vodka girl, aren't you? Tell you what, even better, I'll have a word with this chap, get him to send us up a bottle of vodka. I'll drink the scotch, you drink the vodka, we'll have a party.

Paula No, honestly, it's very nice of you but I'd rather not.

Harry Well, I mean, suit yourself. I mean, nothing like that. We can go to your room if you'd rather.

Paula No, thank you very much all the same.

Harry Ah, well. Not to bother. Just thought you'd care to have a look. Ready for another one?

Paula No, honestly, you've been very kind but I really have to be . . . (*Breaking off as she sees someone in the saloon bar*) Oh, here she is. Bernice!

Harry Hallo, it's your friend, isn't it?

Bernice enters. She is a few years older than Paula

Hallo there. (*He rises*)

Bernice You said in the foyer.

Paula I'm sorry. I met this gentleman, you see. Bernice, this is—er, Harry, isn't it?

Harry Harry Compton, how do you do?

Bernice (*without really taking him in*) How do you do? (*To Paula*) You said you'd be in the foyer.

Paula Well, we're only sitting here just round the corner.

Bernice I didn't see you just round the corner though, did I?

Harry Now, can I get you a drink, Bernice?

Bernice Yes, I'll have a gin and tonic, thank you.

Harry Gin and tonic for Bernice. Another vodka for Paula.

Paula No, no.

Harry (*calling*) Waiter! Can I take your coat, Bernice?

Bernice No, I'll keep it on, thank you. I've been out there half an hour, you know.

Paula I'm sorry.

Bernice Well . . .

Harry Now, now, now. Mustn't quarrel, girls. Waiter.

Bernice (*sitting*) My God, this place is a dump.

Harry (*sitting again by Paula*) Just what we were saying, wasn't it, Paula? After six o'clock, absolutely dead.

Bernice And it was freezing in that shop, what's more.

Harry Yes, it's very bad that. I mean there's no excuse for that. Waiter! Where the hell's he gone to? Hang on, I'll get them myself, it's quicker. Just wait there, girls, I won't be a second. Bernice's thirsty, we can't have that.

Harry goes off to the bar

Bernice Who's your friend?

Paula Oh, you know. He was the one hanging around the counter this morning. The one with all the funny remarks.

Bernice Oh, yes, that's right. That's him. How did you finish up with him?

Paula Because you were late and he caught me standing there on my own in the foyer.

Bernice I was not late. What's he like?

Paula Well, you know . . .

Bernice Let's go then, shall we?

Paula He's buying us a drink now.

Bernice So? We don't want to get stuck with him, do we?

Paula Well, we might as well have the drink now.

Bernice Alright. Then we'll tell him we've got to get back to our hotel. Tell him you're expecting a phone call or something.

Paula That's no good. He thinks we're staying here.

Bernice How did he come to think that?

Paula I don't know, he just did. If we tell him we're at the "Wheatsheaf" he'll only follow us there.

Bernice He won't. (*She produces a scent spray*)

Paula He will.

Bernice Why should he?

Paula Because he's one of those. We've only been talking five minutes and he's been trying to get me up to his bedroom.

Bernice I don't know why you wanted to come to this place anyway. (*She sprays behind her ears*)

Paula Well, Simon said it was good.

Bernice You should know better than to trust Simon. (*She sprays behind her knees*)

Harry returns with drinks

Harry Here we are then, girls. (*Handing them out*) That's the gin, that's the vodka.

Bernice Oh, that's a very big one.

Harry Well. Saves jumping up and down, doesn't it? Now then. Finished your argument? Cheers.

Paula Cheers.

Harry Been out looking at the town, have you?

Bernice Beg your pardon?

Harry Saw you'd got your coat on. Thought you might have been out.

Bernice Oh, yes I went for a walk.

Harry Not much of a place for walks, is it?

Bernice No.

Harry Well, this is the life, isn't it? When I woke up this morning and I knew I was due to come over here, my heart sank I don't mind saying. Then what happens? I finish up with two beautiful girls for company. Just goes to show.

Paula Yes.

Harry Paula and I, we've been chatting away, haven't we, Paula?

Paula Yes.

Harry Right, now. Let's see how I do with Bernice, eh, Paula?

Bernice What?

Harry Now, looking at Bernice—I immediately think of blue. Am I right? You look good in blue, am I right?

Bernice Me?

Harry That's your best colour. Best for you, if you're interested, blue.

Bernice No, I never wear blue.

Paula You've got that blue trouser suit.

Bernice I never wear blue. I hate it.

Harry Well, I could be wrong. It has been known, but it's unusual. You have another look at yourself in blue. See if I'm not right. I'm not talking about royal blue, not a dark blue—more of a pale blue. We've got this dress at the moment, it's in this new material, man-made fibre with ten per cent wool—crease-resistant—it's literally a dress you can roll in a ball, jump on it if you like, give it a shake, put it on, good as new. Now this is a really beautiful blue. A sort of ice blue I suppose you'd call it. Knee length, not a long one. It's got a top rather like you've got on now and I'm not joking, looking at your colouring, Bernice, it would really set that off. Can you see that, Paula, Bernice in blue?

Paula Yes, nice.

Harry She'd look really fantastic. When I saw you this morning at the counter there in amongst all your bottles and perfumes and things, I thought straightaway, that is the girl who could really wear that dress.

Bernice I wouldn't be seen dead in blue.

Harry Ah well. Cheers. No, as I say, I never thought I'd be spending this evening with two gorgeous girls.

Bernice You never know your luck, do you.

Harry Quite right, Bernice, many a true word. Never know your luck. Well. How are we three going to spend this evening?

Bernice Well, we're . . .

Harry Now, now. Plenty of time. Enjoy your drink first, then we'll decide.

The night is young, as they say. So are we. Well, in my case, young in heart. (*He laughs*)

Paula I don't think we'll be wanting to do very much this evening, actually.

Harry All right, fair enough. Let's just stay here then. Fine by me. Have a bite of dinner later.

Bernice Oh no.

Harry It's very good, the restaurant here, you know.

Paula Oh no.

Harry On me. On me. I don't often have the pleasure.

Bernice I don't think actually either of us are very hungry, thank you.

Harry Oh, come on, you've got to eat, you've got to eat. Keep up your strength. No, seriously, I would consider it a great honour. A great honour. Besides, there's nothing worse than eating alone, is there? Be nice if, just for once—the life I lead, I seem to spend my life eating alone.

Paula Well, when you're at home you don't . . .

Harry Ah, well. On those occasions, on those rare occasions . . . Matter of fact, to be frank, I'm not often there. I mean, I don't want to start boring you by talking about myself particularly but, well—let's just say I'm not very often at home. Enough said? Enough said. Cheers. (*Pause*) I mean, don't get me wrong. My wife and I, we're not separated, anything like that. It's just—well, to be perfectly honest she's a lot happier if I'm not at home too much. You might say, we no longer see eye to eye. If you follow my meaning. She's got very strong views on certain matters and, er—well there you are. I mean, I'm—as I was saying only a minute ago to Paula here—I'm by nature—easy going. However, it takes all sorts as they say. It so happens my wife is one of those people who considers that these sort of things cannot be forgiven or forgotten—particularly not forgotten—ever. No matter. No matter how much you may talk to her or apologize to her about it. She's not a woman to take sorry for an answer. So there you are. I live there. On occasions. That's about all. But it's not life. I don't call that life. (*Pause*) Anyway, enough of my problems. (*Pause*) The point is this, if my wife were sitting here now with us all, she would have no claim over me whatsoever. Nor, let's be perfectly honest, would I have on her. Washout. Finish. Waiter, we'll have the same again, please.

The Waiter approaches

Bernice No, thank you very much.

Paula No. Harry, Harry . . .

Harry Waiter! Same again here.

Bernice No, thank you very much. No more, Waiter.

Harry Waiter, we want three more of the same.

Paula No, honestly, Harry . . .

Harry Three more, Waiter, we'll argue it out later.

Waiter Three more, sir.

The Waiter departs

Bernice I don't want any more.

Harry Come on, that's only your first.

Bernice That's all I want.

Harry You've got to catch up with me and Paula, for God's sake.

Bernice I don't have to at all.

Paula It's very kind of you.

Harry Well, he's bringing them now, it's too late. You needn't worry, it's on me. On me. I mean, I'm not a big drinker either, you know. Don't get me wrong. I'm not hooked on it. I can go for weeks without a drink, you know, if I have to. Doesn't bother me in the least. But, for God's sake, if I get the chance of sitting here with two simply stunning-looking creatures the like of which I have never set eyes upon before, believe you me—well, I think it calls for a drink. I don't drink at home, you know. Never drink at home.

Bernice You're never there.

Harry I only drink socially. I only drink to be sociable. No, never been my problem, drink. I've got other problems but drink's not one of them. Thank God. And I do very sincerely thank God. I won't go into my other problems, I don't want to shock you. (*He laughs*) I mean, today, you won't believe that today, I was drinking all lunchtime with a colleague of mine, an old friend, a dear old friend I hadn't seen for a very long time. We had a few together over lunch, I won't deny that and I happened to be in here again when they opened the bar this evening. And I haven't even got a thick head. Would you believe that? Incredible, isn't it?

The Waiter arrives with drinks

Ah. Thank you very much, Waiter. Good man, good man. Room two-four-nine.

Waiter Two-four-nine, sir. Will that be all, sir?

Harry For the time being, thank you very much. (*As the Waiter goes, he calls him back*) Oh, Waiter. Here, here—just a sec. (*Fumbling in his pocket and producing a pound note*) Here's for yourself.

Waiter Oh, that's very kind of you. Thank you very much, sir.

Harry Have one yourself.

Waiter Very kind indeed, sir.

The Waiter goes

Harry Take care of them. They'll take care of you. Cheers.

Bernice (*not touching her drink*) Cheers.

Harry No, I'll tell you both something now. I'll be absolutely honest with you—now, I don't want you to be shocked because the last thing I want to do in this world to you two lovely girls is to shock you but I have to say, you are both of you—now I'm not in any way trying to get off with you, anything like that, you are two of the most amazingly startlingly sexy girls I have ever seen in my life. Now that's no—no—sort of kidding at all. I want you to believe that.

Paula Thank you very much.

Harry No, no, Paula my darling, I want to hear you say you believe that. Will you say very clearly, I believe that.

Paula Yes, we do.

Harry You do believe that, don't you?

Paula Yes.

Bernice gives her a "come on" look

Harry, Bernice has got to meet her uncle at the station

Harry Just a minute, let me finish . . .

Paula She's got to meet her uncle at the station, you see, Harry. The train's due in a few minutes.

Harry No, well I'll get you down to the station, my darling, don't you worry about that. I'll get you a taxi.

Paula No, Harry . . .

Harry I'll buy you a taxi.

Paula We have to go, Harry.

Harry No. Listen, listen, Paula, Paula—Bernice. Listen. This is not in any way an advance, it's not anything like that, please believe that. I mean, I respect you far too much, you see. I respect you as ladies. Look, you see this . . . (*Holding up his room key*) This is a key, right? The key to my room, two-four-nine, which is a very, very nice room, believe me. Now, I'm going to put this key down here in the middle of the table, like that. Now, I'm going to leave it there. I'm not going to try and embarrass you, you see, but it's there. If you want to pick it up, it's there. Entirely up to you. Can't say fairer than that.

Bernice rises

Where are you going?

Bernice We have to go.

Paula tries to rise. Harry pushes her down

Harry Paula, there's the key, you see.

Paula Yes, but you'll need it, Harry.

Harry No, I'll get another one. They have another one at the desk. This is for you.

Bernice Come on.

Harry If you want it, there it is.

Paula Thank you very much, Harry.

Harry Two-four-nine. If you want it, come and get it.

Paula Thank-you, Harry. We have to meet her uncle, you see.

Bernice Paula, are you coming?

Paula Yes, I'm coming. (*She rises*)

Harry (*catching Paula's wrist*) Just a minute, just a minute. Waiter, Waiter.

Paula Wait.

The Waiter arrives

Harry Waiter.

Waiter Yes, sir?

Harry I wonder, Waiter, if you'd do me a favour. These two enchanting young ladies want to go to—where is it?—the railway station—to meet their uncle. Could you arrange them a taxi, do you think?

Waiter The hall porter will get you a taxi, sir.

Harry Ah, well. Would you mind asking him very nicely.

Waiter I'm sorry, sir, I'm not allowed to leave the bar.

Harry Oh, for crying out loud.

Paula It doesn't matter, Harry, don't bother.

Bernice Are you coming?

Harry What's the matter with this place?

Paula We'll walk, Harry, we can walk.

Harry You're not walking. I'm not having you walking, not on your own. I'm going to get you a taxi.

Bernice (*moving in*) We don't want a taxi, thank you.

Harry (*pushing her aside*) Wait there. (*Confidentially*) Paula.

Paula What?

Harry (*pushing the room key into her hand*) Here. You keep this. You understand. It's up to you. It's entirely up to you. I want you to know that. No strings. No strings at all.

Paula Thank you.

Harry (*blundering off*) I won't be a moment. Waiter, I'm relying on you to keep an eye on these magnificent girls.

Waiter I'll do that, sir.

Harry Wait there.

Harry goes through the saloon bar

Bernice Oh my God, I thought we'd never get rid of him.

Paula Awful when they get like that.

Bernice Thought you'd have learnt better by now. We'd better go quick.

Paula We can't. He's just out there.

Bernice (*to the Waiter*) Is there another way out, please?

Waiter Yes, just through there, madam. There's a side door just through to your left.

Bernice Thank you. Right, come on, let's go.

Paula Good night.

Waiter Good night to you, madam.

The girls start to move off by the side door

Oh, madam, excuse me—you won't forget to leave the key, will you?

Paula Oh. Nearly forgot. (*She hands him the key*) Would you mind?
Waiter Not at all, madam. Good night.

Paula and Bernice go

The Waiter slips the key into his pocket and starts to clear the empties, as the Lights fade to a Black-out

BETWEEN MOUTHFULS

A hotel dining-room

Two tables are set apart, each with two chairs. Between them a service table. An IN and OUT door from the kitchens. The main entrance for Guests. The discreet clatter of knives and forks from other invisible diners. The Waiter is finishing arranging his two tables. He wanders over and leans against the service table. At length, Donald Pearce enters, a middle-aged businessman

Waiter (*approaching him*) Good evening, sir.

Pearce Good evening. I have a table for two reserved in the name of Pearce.

Waiter Table for two, sir. Did you make a reservation, sir?

Pearce Yes, I've just said I did.

Waiter Very good, sir. (*He consults the reservations book on the service table*) What name was it, sir?

Pearce Pearce. I've just this minute said so.

Waiter Pearce—with a P, I presume?—ah, yes, sir. (*Indicating the table nearer the door*) Would this one over here suit you, sir?

Pearce No, I don't think it would. I think I'd prefer this one over here.

Waiter Oh, just as you like, sir.

The Waiter leads Pearce over to the table and holds the chair for Pearce, who sits, his back to the rest of the room

Pearce Thank you.

Waiter Just yourself is it, sir?

Pearce No.

Waiter Ah. Someone will be joining you, will they, sir?

Pearce Yes, indeed. That's really rather why I reserved a table for two.

Waiter Right, sir.

The Waiter goes to the service table to collect menus

> *Emma Pearce enters, same age as Pearce, worried and tense. She catches sight of her husband and moves across to join him*

The Waiter hurries across to help her with her chair

Pearce Oh, there you are.

Waiter Good evening, madam.

Mrs Pearce (*sitting*) Thank you. (*To Pearce*) You might have waited for me.

Pearce I had absolutely no idea where you'd got to.

Mrs Pearce You know perfectly well where I was.

Waiter (*handing her a menu*) Thank you, madam.

Mrs Pearce I told you.

Waiter Thank you, sir.

Pearce Thank you.

Mrs Pearce Oh lord. I suppose I've got to read through all this. (*She fumbles in her bag*)

Waiter Would you, madam, or yourself care for a drink before your meal, sir?

Pearce No, we wouldn't, thank you.

Mrs Pearce Oh no, I haven't brought them.

Pearce We may have some wine.

Waiter Right, sir.

Mrs Pearce That's that. I haven't brought them. (*She takes out a cigarette*)

Pearce What?

Mrs Pearce My reading glasses. I've left them at home.

Pearce I suppose that means I've got to read it to you.

The Waiter lights Mrs Pearce's cigarette

Mrs Pearce Unless you want me to guess.

Pearce (*to the Waiter*) Would you bring us an ashtray, please.

Waiter Yes, sir.

Pearce Why the hell you can't keep your glasses permanently in your handbag . . .

The Waiter moves away. As he does so, Pearce's voice fades out. Throughout we hear only that dialogue that the Waiter himself hears when within earshot. Whether or not the Waiter registers the content of what he is hearing apart from remarks directly addressed to him, he never betrays. Pearce continues speaking, but we can no longer hear him. The Waiter fetches the ashtray from the service table, dusts it, and returns to Pearce's table

Mrs Pearce (*fading up*) . . . this afternoon whilst I was reading and I forgot them, that's all.

Pearce All right, all right, all right.

Mrs Pearce (*to the Waiter*) Thank you.

Pearce And we'll have the wine list as well.

Waiter Wine list. Yes, sir.

Pearce Now then, are you listening? Here we go. (*Reading*) Hors d'oeuvres from our trolley, grapefruit cocktail . . . (*He fades out*)

The Waiter returns to the service table for the wine list

Polly and Martin enter, a younger couple

Waiter Good evening, sir. Good evening, madam. Just the two of you, is there?

Martin That's right.

Waiter Have you a reservation, sir?

Martin No, we haven't.

Waiter Just a moment, sir. (*He consults the book*)

Polly I hope there's going to be room.

Martin (*looking round the restaurant*) There'll be room. (*Catching sight of the Pearces*) God, look who's here.

Polly Where?

Martin Over there, look. Donald Pearce and his wife.

Polly Oh.

Martin Better go and say hallo.

Polly No, don't do that.

Martin What?

Polly Let's go somewhere else.

Martin What?

Polly They'll only feel they'll have to ask us to join them. Let's go somewhere else.

Martin I'm not going somewhere else.

Polly They haven't seen us yet. Quick . . .

Martin I'm not going somewhere else. What's the matter with you?

Polly I just don't feel like talking to them.

Martin Why not?

Polly Not now.

Waiter Sorry to keep you, sir. Would this table here be all right, sir?

Martin (*as they follow him to the other table*) You can't expect me to cut my boss dead in a restaurant.

Polly We'll have to pretend we haven't seen them.

Martin It's obvious we've seen them.

Polly Why? They haven't seen us. We could leave now.

The Waiter holds the chair for Polly

Martin I'm not leaving now. (*He sits. To the Waiter*) Thank you. (*To Polly*) What's got into you?

Polly Nothing. (*She sits*)

Waiter Excuse me, sir.

Martin I mean, I thought you always got on with them.

Polly They're all right.

Waiter Excuse me, sir.

Martin You've always been quite happy to talk to them in the past.

Waiter Would you care for a drink before your meal, sir?

Martin You used to be perfectly happy . . . (*To the Waiter*) No, thank you —perfectly happy to go round when they invited us.

Polly Not tonight. I don't feel like sitting down . . . (*She fades out*)

The Waiter returns to the service table and picks up the wine list. He moves to the Pearces' table with it

Pearce (*fading up*) . . . Dover sole meuniere. Lobster thermidor. Lobster americaine brackets when in season. Scampi—all sorts of scampi— grilled halibut . . . (*He fades out*)

The Waiter has slipped the wine list down beside Pearce's elbow and departed. He returns to his service table, takes up two menus and crosses to Martin's table

Polly . . . seen you for three weeks. I'd rather like it if we were just on our own.

Martin I'm not the one who went away.

Polly All the same . . .

Martin I mean, you're the one who went off on holiday. I didn't go off on holiday.

Polly You could have done. (*Taking her menu*) Thank you.

Martin I couldn't, I told you. Old Pearce there—(*taking his menu*)—thank you—old Pearce there landed me with enough work to last me a year.

Polly That wasn't my fault, Martin . . .

Martin I'm not saying it was. I was merely explaining why . . .

The Waiter departs. He edges towards the Pearces' table with his order pad

Pearce . . . grilled pork chops, tournedos à la Crowne—whatever that may be—steak diane, grilled fillet steak brackets when available. Rump steak—Garni . . .

The Waiter withdraws and leans against the service table, waiting. After a moment, he moves again to Martin's table to see if any decision has been made there

Martin . . . book a holiday at a time when you know I'm going to be very busy.

Polly Because if I waited for you not to be busy I'd never get a holiday at all.

Martin Come on, darling. This chap wants us to order.

Waiter No hurry, sir, no hurry.

Polly I mean, it was either a case of my taking a holiday on my own or not having a . . .

The Waiter wanders back to the Pearces

Pearce . . . roast Aylesbury duckling with orange sauce. Roast spring chicken with stuffing. Roast turkey with cranberry sauce . . .

The Waiter withdraws. Martin signals for the Waiter. The Waiter moves to Martin's table

Polly . . . enjoy going on holiday on my own.

Martin Waiter, what's the Soup of the Day?

Waiter (*checking over Martin's shoulder*) Er —minestrone, sir.

Martin (*unenthusiastically*) Oh.

Martin and Polly ponder their menus. The Waiter hovers

How was the trip back?

Polly Not bad. Had to be at the airport at seven this morning. We got to Heathrow at ten . . .

Martin Sorry I couldn't meet you.
Polly I didn't expect you to.
Martin Our sales meeting went on till lunchtime.

Pearce signals and mimes Waiter

Waiter Yes, sir?

The Waiter moves across from Martin's table to Pearce's

Pearce Waiter, what is the Soup of the Day?
Waiter Minestrone, sir.
Pearce Oh.

Pause

Waiter Do you wish to order now, sir?
Mrs Pearce Do you do Eggs Benedict?
Waiter (*doubtfully; looking over Pearce's shoulder*) Eggs Benedict,
    madam . . .
Pearce I should imagine that if they did Eggs Benedict, they'd have put
    Eggs Benedict on the menu.
Waiter I don't think we do, madam.
Mrs Pearce I was only asking.
Pearce I mean, I read you the menu very distinctly. I didn't read out Eggs
    Benedict, did I?
Mrs Pearce I don't know.
Pearce But I've only just this minute finished reading it to you.
Mrs Pearce I don't know, I wasn't listening.
Pearce (*taking a deep breath*) I think we need a few more minutes to
    decide, Waiter.
Waiter Very good, sir.
Pearce I suppose you want me to read it to you all over again . . .

The Waiter hovers back near Martin and Polly

Polly . . . marvellous the whole time. Baking hot. And it's a beautiful
    island.
Martin (*uninterestedly*) Yes. Sounds it. (*Seeing the Waiter*) Ah. Now then.
    So far we've got one pâté—one smoked trout. And you were . . .? ˉ
Waiter (*writing*) Pâté maison—smoked trout.
Polly Is the lobster fresh?
Waiter Oh yes, madam. I can recommend it.
Polly Then I'll have Thermidor with a green salad.
Martin Poulet estragon for me.
Waiter Poulet estragon—thermidor. Would you care to see the wine list,
    sir?
Martin Might as well. My wife has just returned from the sunny Mediter-
    ranean. She's probably got the taste after three weeks.
Waiter Very nice, too, madam. Excuse me a moment, sir.

The Waiter moves across again to the Pearces

Mrs Pearce . . . the moment you come back, you start.

Pearce I'm not starting again. I was merely saying . . . (*Seeing the Waiter*) Yes?

Waiter I just wondered if you were ready with your order yet, sir.

Pearce No indeed, we are not ready with our order yet. We will let you know when we are.

Waiter Very good, sir.

Mrs Pearce Every single time you come back from somewhere, you're absolutely . . .

The Waiter collects the wine list from the service table

Martin . . . it was your idea.

Polly I didn't know they were going to be here, did I?

Martin It was your idea we came out.

Polly Since the children were away, I thought it would be nice.

Martin It was a lovely idea. Enjoy it.

Polly Yes, but I didn't know they were going to be here, did I . . .

Pearce (*calling*) Waiter!

The Waiter returns to Pearce

Waiter Sir?

Pearce You will be pleased to hear that we have at last decided. Pencil at the ready. Here we go. One potted shrimps—one grapefruit cocktail and if it has a maraschino cherry on it, we don't want it. One Dover sole meunière off the bone—one rump steak, just this side of medium rare . . .

Waiter (*scribbling furiously*) Just a minute, sir—Dover sole off the bone— rump steak, medium rare . . . Have you decided on a wine, sir?

Pearce Oh—yes. (*He opens the list*) White? Emma? White, do you want white?

Mrs Pearce I don't mind either way. I only want half a glass.

Pearce Well, just say red or white?

Mrs Pearce I honestly don't mind. (*She looks out front*)

Pearce Red, then.

Mrs Pearce turns sharply and glares at him

Ah, now. What have you got in the Italian line?

Waiter I think they're at the back here, sir. The wine waiter's not on at the moment, otherwise . . .

Pearce Ah yes, here we are, Italian. We had a very very reasonable one at the hotel where we stayed.

Mrs Pearce I thought you went there to work.

Pearce I did go there to work. I had to stop occasionally. Now then.

Mrs Pearce My husband's been overworking in Italy, poor thing . . .

Pearce No, you don't seem to have it.

Mrs Pearce I don't know how you managed to work in all that blazing sunshine.

Pearce A bottle of this one here, the—er—one-oh-four.

Waiter Oh right, sir. The—er—one-oh-four. Yes, sir.

Mrs Pearce How on earth did you manage to cope for three whole weeks . . .?

The Waiter goes out through to the kitchens and after a second, returns. He takes up some cutlery, places it on a tray and crosses to Martin's table

Martin . . . last six months are beginning to move. Somebody up there seems to have our interests at heart, anyway.

Waiter Smoked trout, madam?

Martin No, that's me—and not before time, as far as I'm concerned. Old Pearce was back this afternoon, full of the joys of spring, anyway. I don't know what he got up to in Rome but he seems to have had a good time of it.

The Waiter exchanges some of Polly's and Martin's cutlery, replacing it with a fish knife and fork

Polly I thought he went on business.

Martin I can't believe it took him three weeks to get a contract signed. I know the Italians are difficult . . . mind you, I think if I was married to Emma Pearce, I'd chase off to Rome.

Polly Don't stare.

Martin It's all right, he's got his back to us. And she's as blind as a bat. No, he probably had some little Italian señora lined up there. He always likes to mix his business with a bit of . . .

The Waiter goes to Pearce's table

Waiter Potted shrimps, sir?

Pearce Thank you.

Waiter And a steak for madam?

Pearce No, that's for me as well.

A pause while the Waiter exchanges cutlery, replacing Mrs Pearce's with a fish knife and fork, and Pearce's with an outer fish knife and fork and a steak knife

Mrs Pearce Well, I'm sorry, I don't believe you.

Pearce That's up to you. (*Pause*) That's what I was doing.

Mrs Pearce I'm sorry, I think you're a liar.

The Waiter crosses to Martin and Polly

Martin . . . and the problem was to re-allocate staff work schedules so that everyone was guaranteed at least one day off in three whilst guaranteeing normal production.

Polly Yes.

Waiter Excuse me, sir.

Martin Which was one hell of a problem. Yes?

Waiter Have you chosen a wine, sir?

Martin (*picking up the wine list*) Oh yes—you see, as soon as you say, lost men off the assembly section, you had to insure you had sufficient man-power to tide you over the entire three-day period without any noticeable shrinkage in labour effectiveness.

Polly Martin, he's waiting to know what wine.

Martin Oh yes. Do you do a carafe?

Waiter Yes, sir.

Martin A carafe of white. Not too sweet.

Waiter Carafe of the white, sir

Martin Anyway, we managed it. We put in the report and Donald Pearce is over the moon. I mean, he only had time to glance at it this afternoon but . . .

The Waiter goes into the kitchens

The Pearces sit in silence. Martin chatters on to Polly

The Waiter returns with the Pearces' first courses, grapefruit cocktail, potted shrimps, plate of toast. He crosses to Pearce's table

Waiter Grapefruit cocktail, madam?

Mrs Pearce Thank you.

Waiter Potted shrimps, sir.

Pearce Thank you.

Mrs Pearce I'm sorry, I think you're lying.

Waiter Beg your pardon, madam? Oh, I'm sorry, madam, I beg your pardon. Toast is there, sir.

The Waiter returns to the kitchens

The Pearces eat, Martin continues to talk

The Waiter returns with Martin's and Polly's first courses. He goes to their table

Martin . . . so in the end I did the only thing possible. I took on entire responsibility for the whole A, D and J project. Took on both jobs. Did the lot myself.

Polly Yes, I know, you told me this before, Martin.

The Waiter serves her with pâté

Thank you.

Martin When did I tell you? (*He leans forward over the table*)

The Waiter tries unsuccessfully to slip the plate under Martin's hands

Polly I've only been away three weeks, you know.

Martin What time are we picking up the kids?

Polly I told Gran we'd be there in time for lunch.

Martin Ah well, end of peace and quiet. (*He leans back*)

The Waiter quickly slides Martin's plate into place

Thank you.

Polly Did you miss them?

Martin I honestly haven't had a moment to miss anyone, love. Not even you.

Polly I missed them dreadfully.

Waiter (*fiddling at the table*) Toast is just there, madam.

Polly Thank you

Martin Oh, did I tell you, Graham Shotter finally got that job in Glasgow.

Polly Oh, did he . . .

The Waiter goes to the kitchen, returning with both the carafe and Pearce's wine. He puts the carafe down on the service table, wipes the bottle, shakes it upside down, then takes it to Pearce's table and holds it out for his inspection

Waiter Sir. The one-oh-four, sir.

Pearce Oh yes. (*He reads the label very carefully, muttering all the words to himself including the name of the shippers*) Righto, yes.

Waiter Th·nk you, sir.

The Waiter produces a cork-screw from his pocket and starts to open the bottle by their table

Pearce Did you get someone in to look at that radiator in the bedroom?

Mrs Pearce They said they'd come on Tuesday.

Pearce Oh.

Mrs Pearce He said it sounded as if it needed a new part.

Pearce That's out.

The Waiter pulls out the cork with a "pop"

I'm not paying for a new part. I'm not wasting money on that.

Mrs Pearce Just on holidays. (*She lights another cigarette*)

The Waiter pours a little wine into Pearce's glass

Pearce Are you deliberately trying to annoy me this evening?

Waiter Would you care to try it, sir?

Pearce Oh . . . (*He sips his glass*) Bit on the chill side. It'll do. Go ahead.

Waiter Thank you, sir.

The Waiter starts to pour wine for Mrs Pearce

Mrs Pearce That's enough, thank you.

Waiter Thank you, madam.

Pearce Are you eating that or just leaving it?

Mrs Pearce Leaving it.

The Waiter pours Pearce the rest of his glass and puts the bottle on the table

Waiter I'll leave it here, sir. Finished, madam?
Mrs Pearce Yes, thank you.
Waiter Was it all right for you, madam?
Mrs Pearce Beautiful. I'm just not very hungry.
Waiter (*removing her plate*) Thank you, madam.
Pearce I don't see any point in ordering food if you're not going to eat it . . .

The Waiter returns to the service table, picks up the carafe of wine and crosses to Martin and Polly's table

Polly I just think it's a terrific cheek, that's all.
Martin No, honestly, love, it isn't really I—thank you—

The Waiter starts to pour wine for Polly. She picks up her glass while he is still pouring

The quality of the wife is frightfully important. If you've got a top executive virtually responsible for what?—two or three hundred men sometimes—it's vitally important that he's married to the right woman.
Polly Why?
Martin Well, that he has a stable relationship. That she's suddenly not going to walk out on him.

The Waiter picks up Martin's glass and fills it, so that Martin cannot touch it until he has finished pouring

Polly She's going to take no part in his work, is she?
Martin Well, hardly, no.
Polly Then I think the firm ought to mind its own bloody business, I'm sorry . . .

The Waiter moves away, Pearce finishes. The Waiter moves in to take his plate

Mrs Pearce I said, who is she?
Pearce Who is who?
Mrs Pearce Who is she?

Pearce opens his mouth to reply then becomes aware of the waiter. The Waiter takes away his plate and puts it on the service table. He sees Polly and Martin have finished and goes to remove their plates

Polly . . . what I'm saying is, that as far as I'm concerned, you could be manufacturing—marmalade. You spend all day in the office, you work at home most of the night, you never talk to the children and I don't even know half the time what it is that you're doing.
Martin Look, darling, you wouldn't understand if I told you . . .

The Waiter takes the empty plates to the kitchen

Pearce and Mrs Pearce are having a short, terse conversation. Martin talks agitatedly. Polly looks slightly desperate

The Waiter returns with the Pearces' second course: rump steak for him, Dover sole for her, and vegetables. He goes to their table

Pearce I don't think this is quite the occasion for this sort of conversation, do you?

Mrs Pearce I can't think of any better time.

Pearce In a public restaurant.

Mrs Pearce Why not?

Waiter Dover sole, madam.

Mrs Pearce Thank you.

Pearce I don't see any point in causing a scene . . .

Mrs Pearce I am not causing a scene. I asked you a perfectly normal question. Who is this woman?

Waiter Rump steak, sir.

Pearce What does it matter?

Mrs Pearce Because I want to know.

Pearce Who said there was anyone, anyway?

Mrs Pearce Oh, come along, darling, I am not a fool. I am not a bloody fool.

Pearce Would you mind lowering your voice.

Mrs Pearce I will not lower my voice.

Waiter Runner beans, madam?

Mrs Pearce No, thank you.

Waiter Carrots, madam?

Mrs Pearce No, thank you. I want nothing else.

Waiter No potatoes either, madam?

Mrs Pearce (*shrilly*) Nothing else.

Waiter Very good, madam. (*He moves round to Pearce*)

Pearce (*to Mrs Pearce, fiercely*) Could you kindly try and control yourself.

Waiter Runner beans for you, sir?

Pearce (*snarling at him*) Yes please.

Mrs Pearce Well, I'll tell you one thing, darling, if I ever get my hands on the little whore, I'll wring her neck.

Pearce Do you mind, do you mind.

Waiter Carrots, sir?

Pearce Yes.

Mrs Pearce You can tell the little bitch that from me.

Waiter Potatoes, sir?

Pearce No. No potatoes. Nothing else.

Waiter Very good, sir.

Pearce Nothing else, at all.

Waiter Right, sir.

The Waiter moves away and returns to the kitchens

Both tables are in a fair state of animation

The Waiter returns with Polly's and Martin's main courses: lobster, chicken, salad dressing, salad, vegetables. He moves to their table

Polly ... that's what it boils down to. I'm not in the slightest bit interested in your work and you don't give a damn what I'm up to. There we are. We haven't one thing in common.

Martin Oh, come on, I don't know.

The Waiter serves Polly's lobster

Polly Thank you.

Martin I'm interested in what you're up to.

Polly Really?

Martin Of course ...

Polly Nonsense.

Martin It's not nonsense at all.

Waiter (*serving*) Poulet estragon, sir.

Polly These last three weeks I was away, were you the slightest bit interested in where I was?

Martin I know where you were.

Polly Do you?

Martin You were in—wherever it is—Majorca.

Polly I was not in Majorca, darling, as it happens. I was in Rome.

Waiter Vegetables, sir?

Martin Er—just carrots. Rome? What were you doing in Rome?

Polly I was with Donald Pearce.

Martin Donald Pearce—that's fine, thank you—what were you doing with Donald Pearce?

Polly I spent three weeks with Donald Pearce in a hotel in Rome.

Martin My God. (*He puts his head in his hands on the table*)

Waiter Potatoes, sir?

Martin Oh my God.

Waiter (*bending right down to speak to Martin*) Excuse me, sir.

Polly (*to the Waiter*) No, he doesn't.

Waiter Oh, right, madam.

Polly (*to Martin*) I'm sorry.

Waiter Sorry, madam?

Polly Nothing.

Waiter Oh, sorry, madam. Green salad.

Martin Oh my God.

Polly Thank you.

Waiter French dressing, madam?

Polly Yes, just a little.

Martin How could you do it?

Polly I don't know. I'm sorry. I felt—I don't know ...

Martin You realize what you've done?

Polly It's not important, darling, it's all over. That's why I told you.

Martin It may be all over for you. What happens when she finds out?

Polly Who?

Martin Emma Pearce. You realize what's going to happen to me.
Polly What?
Martin I'll be out on my ear. As soon as Emma Pearce gets wind of—oh, damn it. If you were going to choose someone why the hell did it have to be Donald Pearce? That's it, don't you see? That's the end of everything. The end of my prospects of promotion. I shall probably be forced to resign.
Polly Is that what's worrying you?
Martin Of course it's what's worrying me.
Waiter Is that sufficient for you, madam?
Polly Oh, for crying out loud, I can't believe it—I just can't believe it. (*She stands, pushing back her chair*)
Martin Where are you going?
Polly Don't you care anything for me? Nothing at all?
Martin Where are you going?
Polly I'm going to be physically sick.

Polly storms out

Waiter Was everything all right for madam, sir?
Martin Yes, it was fine, fine. Thank you very much
Waiter Thank you, sir.

The Waiter moves away and crosses to the Pearces' table with the intention of topping up the wine glasses, trying not to be noticed

Pearce For the last time, will you pull yourself together.
Mrs Pearce I'll kill her when I see her, I'll kill her.
Pearce Don't be so stupid. (*Seeing the Waiter, sharply*) What do you want?
Waiter I was—just going to pour some more wine, sir.
Pearce We can do that ourselves. Go away.
Waiter Just as you like, sir. (*He starts to go*)
Mrs Pearce Waiter.
Waiter Madam?
Mrs Pearce (*indicating her plate*) You can take this away.
Waiter Have you finished, madam?
Mrs Pearce Yes, it was quite delicious, thank you very much. (*She gets up*) Excuse me.
Waiter Was everything all right, madam?
Mrs Pearce Perfectly. It's just I'm afraid I'm unable to enjoy a meal with a man who turns out to be a deceitful, lecherous liar.

Mrs Pearce flips Pearce's plate into his lap. Pearce leaps up

Mrs Pearce goes out of the restaurant hurriedly, blowing her nose. She passes by Martin without seeing him

Martin, sitting stunned, does not see her

Pearce (*dabbing at his trousers with his napkin*) Oh, for the love of mike.
Waiter I'll get a cloth, sir. Just a minute.
Pearce Look at this, look at this. Where's the Gents? I'll have to mop up.

Martin rises

Waiter Just through here, sir. I'll show you.

The Waiter leads Pearce to the door past Martin's table. Martin has risen

Pearce Damn fool thing to do. What a damn . . . (*He bumps into Martin*) Excuse me, I—good God, hallo, Chalmers.
Martin Oh, hallo, Mr Pearce.
Pearce I didn't know you were here. Excuse me, I've just had a bit of a mishap.
Martin Oh, good heavens, yes.
Pearce Having a night out, are you?
Martin Yes, yes, that's right.
Pearce So are we. Well, have to unwind once in a while, don't you?
Martin Rather, rather . . .
Pearce Are you still eating, or are you . . . ?
Martin No, I was just . . .
Pearce Well, I'll tell you what. I've just got to have a quick mop up in the Gents. Won't be a second. Then—fancy a quick brandy in the bar?
Martin Oh, that would be very nice indeed, Mr Pearce.
Pearce Just a quick one . . . (*To the Waiter, who is still mopping at his trouser*) All right, that'll do, Waiter, thank you. Could you bring the bill through to the bar, please.
Waiter Yes, of course, sir.
Pearce Oh, and you can put them all on to one if you like.
Martin Oh, that's most generous of you, sir.
Pearce Not at all, not at all. I think after all that stalwart work you've done on that report I probably owe you a meal, don't I?
Martin Oh, I don't know about that . . .

The Waiter moves out of earshot. Pearce claps Martin on the back. The Waiter starts to clear the Pearces' table

Pearce and Martin leave the restaurant, Pearce with his hand on Martin's shoulder, both laughing and talking animatedly

The Waiter looks out front, as—

the CURTAIN *falls*

GOSFORTH'S FÊTE

A tea tent

One long trestle table, the odd bench or collapsible chair. In one corner near one of the entrances, a jerry-rigged rather large valve-type amplifier with wires leading from it to outside. Another entrance at the other end of the table

Milly, a fresh-faced pink woman, staggers in with a box of teacups. She is wearing an overall-coat. She dumps the cups on the table. She attempts to assess the number in the box without removing them. She is involved with this when Emma Pearce comes in through the other entrance. She is now smartly turned out in a feather hat, light raincoat, white gloves with smart matching bag and shoes

Mrs Pearce Excuse me.
Milly I'm sorry, I'm afraid we're not serving teas for another two hours. Can I help you at all?
Mrs Pearce Well, I'm Emma Pearce.
Milly Em—oh golly. Councillor Mrs Pearce.
Mrs Pearce That's right.
Milly Oh. Golly. Um. Well. Has nobody met you?
Mrs Pearce No. I saw one or two people. They seemed rather busy.
Milly Oh, yes . . .
Mrs Pearce I parked just in the lane there. Is that alright?
Milly Fine. I should think. I'm afraid we're all a bit behindhand.
Mrs Pearce Yes. Well, Mr—er—Gosfirth . . .
Milly Gosforth, yes . . .
Mrs Pearce He did say in his letter two-fifteen.
Milly He should be about—somewhere. He was. I'm Milly Carter.

They shake hands

Mrs Pearce How do you do.
Milly It's very nice of you to come.
Mrs Pearce Quite all right.
Milly Is your husband any better?
Mrs Pearce Better?
Milly Yes. Hasn't he been ill?
Mrs Pearce No.
Milly Oh. I thought that's why he couldn't come. Sorry.
Mrs Pearce No. It's just he had some business to see to. He couldn't get away. At the last minute.

Milly Oh, I see.

Mrs Pearce So you'll have to make do with me, I'm afraid.

Milly Yes . . . Oh, no. Not at all. We all tremendously appreciate your being here. Really. Super. Really.

Mrs Pearce Thank you.

Milly And it's for a jolly good cause.

Mrs Pearce Yes, indeed.

Milly I mean, it's just what this place needs—a new village hall. Did you pass the old one on your way here? You probably did.

Mrs Pearce Was that the building on the . . . ?

Milly Yes. Just along the lane there. I mean, frankly it's an eyesore. It was put up during the war. All corrugated iron. If you're holding a meeting and it rains, you might as well save your breath.

Mrs Pearce Oh dear. The weather looks a little threatening today.

Milly Yes. I do hope it doesn't rain. I mean, we can house quite a lot of our activities in the marquee over there—or even in this tea tent if the worst came to the worst, but there's things like Mr Stokes's Wolf Cubs' P.T. display—you couldn't fit that in here for instance.

Mrs Pearce Were those Wolf Cubs, all those little boys out there in gym vests?

Milly Yes. Were they behaving themselves?

Mrs Pearce They were throwing stones at a caravan. I told them to stop it.

Milly Oh lord, good for you. They won't take a blind bit of notice. They're all little horrors. Every one of them. But thanks for trying. No, you see it's vital we get a good attendance. Absolutely vital. Mr Gosforth has worked tirelessly. I'm o/c teas. Tea lady for the day. I usually teach at the school.

Mrs Pearce Oh, how interesting.

Milly Quite a challenge, I can tell you. Most of the children round here are as thick as two planks. We don't seem to have any budding village genius . . .

The sound of Gosforth's voice is heard off, through a loud-hailer, shouting "Keep off there, you boys"

Oh, here's Mr Gosforth.

Mrs Pearce Ah.

Gosforth enters. He is beery-faced, shirtsleeved, perspiring, at present a born leader of men. In one hand, he carries a battery-operated loud-hailer, in the other, a plastic carrier-bag filled with clinking bottles. He looks as if he is in the thick of battle. As soon as he has entered, he turns and glares out through the tent entrance

Gosforth (*bellowing through his loud-hailer*) Will all you Wolf Cubs come down off that scaffolding at once. This is your last warning. (*Lowering the loud-hailer and turning into the tent*) Bloody little vandals, swarming all over it like . . . (*Seeing Mrs Pearce*) Ah. . .

Milly Mr Gosforth, this is Councillor Pearce.

Gosforth Oh good lord, hallo. (*He puts the loud-hailer on the table and shakes hands*)

Mrs Pearce How do you do.

Gosforth Gordon Gosforth. So nice of you to come. Sorry I wasn't there to meet you. Been having a bit of a guy-rope crisis.

Mrs Pearce Oh dear.

Gosforth We rented both these damn tents, you see. Didn't really open them up until today. Didn't have the space. When we do, we find half the guy ropes are missing off the main marquee—this one's safe enough —had to do an emergency job. Not a window left in the district with any sash cord. (*He laughs*) Now, the curriculum goes as follows. Two-thirty p.m. we plan to kick-off. I'll give you a short introduction— needn't be too long—as soon as you've finished—up strikes the band— got them coming over from Hadforth—they should be here—why aren't they?—then if you can mingle about a bit if you don't mind a spot of mingling—have a go at bowling for the pig—just seen Fred Crake's trailer so the pig's arrived safely, thank God—roll a few pennies and all that sort of thing—then, at three-thirty—if you can stay till then—I hope you can—Second Little Pendon Wolf Cubs' P.T. Display, organized by Stewart Stokes—that should go on for about half-an-hour—four o'clock tea, courtesy Milly Carter and assorted ladies—four-thirty, soon as they've swallowed their biscuits—novelty races, fathers' race, mothers' race, three-legged grandfathers' race, all that sort of rubbish—five-thirty to six—final round-off with an organized sing-song with the Hadforth Band—has the Reverend managed to get the song-sheets run off?—ten pounds to a quid he hasn't—six o'clock all pack up, dismantle tents—seven-thirty all cleared away because old Swales wants the field back for his cows first thing in the morning. Hope you can stay for a bit of the fun.

Mrs Pearce Yes.

Gosforth Sure you'll want to. Milly, where is that blasted man Fair-child?

Milly He said he'd be back. He had to go on a call.

Gosforth He had better be back. Not a solitary thing is working. (*To Mrs Pearce*) Penalty of having a local quack who is also the electrical expert. (*He indicates the amplifier*) Rigged up the entire sound system— got all the wires down—microphones—amplifier there, you see—loud-speakers, the lot. Only trouble is, not a bloody thing's working. Now he's taken off on some emergency.

Mrs Pearce Oh dear.

Gosforth Oh dear, indeed. If he doesn't fix it when you make your speech nobody'll hear a word you're saying . . .

There is a rumble of thunder

That sounds ominous. Milly, my darling . . .

Milly Yes, Gordon?

Gosforth (*handing her the carrier-bag*) These are some prizes for the races. Half a dozen bottles of sherry. Could you hide them behind the counter where the Cubs can't get at them. (*To Mrs Pearce*) Advantages of running a pub. Ready-made prizes always to hand. (*He catches sight of something going on outside the tent behind her*) Excuse me a minute. (*Snatching up the loud-hailer and shouting through it*) Reverend, over here. Reverend, would you mind . . . (*Lowering the loud-hailer, to Mrs Pearce*) Useful gadget this. Saves the voice. Would you like a look round before we start, Councillor Mrs Pearce? We may be a few minutes. I think you'll find it impressive. What there is of it so far, anyway.

Mrs Pearce Lovely.

The Vicar enters, laughing. He laughs a lot, especially when he is nervous

Vicar (*laughing*) Hallo there. Bad news, I'm afraid, Gosforth.
Gosforth What's happened?
Vicar I've been finally let down on the song-sheets, I'm afraid.
Gosforth (*clasping his head*) Oh—(*inaudibly*)—help us. Pardon the language.
Vicar No, the man who owned the duplicator has gone out of business.
Gosforth Oh well. Delete community singing. Insert community humming.
Vicar (*laughing*) Community humming, I like that . . . (*Seeing Mrs Pearce*) Oh, I beg your . . .
Gosforth I'm so sorry. Councillor Mrs Pearce, this is John Braithwaite, our vicar.
Mrs Pearce How do you do.

They shake hands

Vicar How do you do. Very kind of you—to turn out. And how is your husband? Better, I hope.
Mrs Pearce He's not ill.
Vicar Oh dear, seriously?
Mrs Pearce No, he's not ill.
Vicar Oh, I beg your pardon. I thought you said he got ill. He's not ill. That's better.
Mrs Pearce Yes.
Vicar There's a big difference between not ill and got ill, isn't there? No, we don't want to get those two confused.
Gosforth John, I wonder if you'd like to show Councillor Mrs Pearce the lie of the land. Take her for a turn round the tombola.
Vicar Of course. Delighted.
Gosforth If you'll excuse me, Councillor—I think I'll have to pitch in to this public address system—see what I can do with it myself.
Mrs Pearce Yes, of course.
Gosforth Twelve loudspeakers strung all the way round the field and not a squeak out of any of them.
Vicar Would you care to follow me, Councillor?

Mrs Pearce Yes, of course. See you later.

Mrs Pearce exits

Gosforth Yes indeed. And Vicar, would you tell those confounded Wolf
Cubs to come down off that scaffolding. It was only built for loud-
speakers, you see.
Vicar I will, I will.
Gosforth They're not designed to take that sort of weight, you see.
Vicar Quite. Point taken.

The Vicar exits

Gosforth In fact, as far as I can make out, they're not designed to take
any sort of weight. Now then, how's my little Milly, all right?
Milly I think we're all right. Old Mr Durban is bringing the tea urn over
in a minute.
Gosforth Splendid. Now then . . .

Thunder

Oh, grief. Hark at that. Now then, where do I start with this lot. (*He
looks at the amplifier on the floor*) The amplifier seems to be working
okay. (*He turns on the light*) Well, anyway, the light's on . . .
Milly Gordon . . .
Gosforth (*involved*) Just a second, lovey . . . I'd better start at the business
end and work round. Loose connection somewhere. That's all it can
be. (*He starts to examine the mike plugs and lead, testing them from
time to time*) Hallo, hallo, one, two, three, four, five.
Milly Gordon, have you a minute, please?
Gosforth Hallo, hallo. Where the hell's that damn fiancé of yours got to?
Milly I don't know.
Gosforth Well, I wish he'd stick around. He could have helped me sort
this out. He's never around when you need him. Those damn Wolf
Cubs of his are running amok.
Milly Gordon, have you got a minute? Please . . .
Gosforth (*sitting on a chair, still fiddling with the mike*) Darling girl, does
it look as if I've got a minute?
Milly It's frightfully urgent, Gordon.
Gosforth All right, old girl, go ahead. I'll just keep fiddling.
Milly Well . . . (*She pauses*)
Gosforth Uh-huh . . .
Milly It's really rather awful. It does seem terribly as if perhaps I might be
pregnant.
Gosforth Oh yes.
Milly Yes.

*Gosforth drops the mike, as he realizes what she has said. The jolt causes the
mike to become live. We hear, distantly, their voices echoing away on a*

series of loudspeakers. They alone, in their concern, remain unaware of this

Gosforth Did you say pregnant?
Milly I'm frightfully sorry.
Gosforth Me?
Milly There's no-one else it could have been, Gordon.
Gosforth Oh my God. (*He rises, with the mike*)
Milly I'm really awfully sorry. What are we going to do?
Gosforth Well . . .
Milly What am I going to say to Stewart?
Gosforth Oh . . .
Milly He'll be dreadfully upset
Gosforth Yes, I can see he might, yes.
Milly He might refuse to marry me.
Gosforth Yes, I can see he might, yes.
Milly (*her lip trembling*) I don't know what to do.
Gosforth Now, easy, easy, Milly. (*He puts his arm round her*) Now, you're absolutely sure.
Milly Yes.
Gosforth Yes. Well. This needs thinking about.
Milly What's Stewart going to say when he finds out? What's it going to do to him? Everyone knows we're engaged. How's he going to face his Cubs?
Gosforth Well, he's a good bloke. He's a Scout, isn't he, after all. He's pretty decent. Now listen, Milly, we must just get through today first. Then we'll talk about it. You see?
Milly Yes.
Gosforth Don't worry.
Milly No.
Gosforth You're not to worry, we'll sort it out. But first things first. You get your tea organized and I'll see if I can get this wretched thing to— one, two, three—ah, success, it's working—don't know what it was I did but I—ah . . .

They look at each other, appalled

Milly How long's it been on for?
Gosforth Very good point.

Stewart Stokes enters in full Scout kit. Normally a pink young man—he is now red with fury

Milly Stewart . . . !
Stewart You bastard, Gosforth . . .
Gosforth Hallo, old boy.
Stewart You complete and utter bastard, Gosforth.
Gosforth Now keep calm, Stokes.
Stewart I'm going to kill you, Gosforth.

Gosforth Stokes, keep calm.

Stewart With my bare hands.

Gosforth I warn you, Stokes, this thing is live.

Stewart Well, switch it off, you coward, switch it off.

Gosforth I don't know how to switch it off.

Stewart Haven't you done enough? How do you think it feels to hear the news that my fiancée is pregnant by another man? Isn't that bad enough? But when you publicly announce it over four acres of field . . . in front of all my Cubs . . .

Gosforth I say, Stewart, I'm sorry.

Stewart There are Brownies out there as well, you know.

Gosforth This is still on, Stewart, this is still on.

Stewart throws down his Scout's pole, seizes the mike and tries to wrest it from Gosforth's hand

Stewart And turn it off! Turn it off!

Gosforth Steady, steady, steady. This thing is still on. Milly, turn it off. Turn it off!

Milly Wait, wait, stop it. (*She switches the amplifier off*) It's off now. It's off.

Gosforth Thank God.

Milly Stewart, we'll have to talk about this later.

Stewart I do not want to talk about this later. I do not want to talk about it at all.

Milly Stewart, please. It's no help to anyone getting in a state.

Gosforth She's quite right, Stewart old man, she's quite right.

Stewart (*collapsing in a chair, almost in tears*) Four acres—four acres . . .

Gosforth Steady, Stewart, old boy, steady. We'll sort it out, I promise. We'll all sit down later and sort it out. Milly, crack open one of those bottles of mine, would you? Give him a glass of sherry.

Stewart I don't drink. You know I never drink.

Gosforth Well, you're in need of one now. Milly . . .

Milly Yes, just a minute.

Milly opens a bottle and pours some into a cup

The Vicar sticks his head into the tent

Vicar Excuse me.

Gosforth Yes, Vicar?

Vicar Were you aware that your ill-tidings were being broadcast abroad?

Gosforth Yes. Thank you, John, we were aware.

Vicar I see. Oh dear. I'm dreadfully sorry . . .

Gosforth Yes. Thank you, John, thank you.

The Vicar goes

Oh well, sorry, Milly. There goes your reputation as spinster of this parish.

Stewart That's not funny, Gosforth.
Gosforth Sorry, old boy, sorry.
Milly (*bringing over the cup and bottle of sherry*) Here . . .
Gosforth Here we are. Drink up, old boy, drink up.

Stewart drinks reluctantly

Milly Perhaps he ought to lie down in the first-aid tent.
Stewart I don't want to lie down.
Gosforth The first-aid tent isn't up yet. Someone's swiped one of their poles.
Stewart I've got things I have to do.
Milly What?
Stewart I haven't finished the platform.

It starts to rain

Gosforth You haven't? Oh lord.
Milly What platform?
Gosforth The platform upon which Councillor Mrs Pearce is supposed to make her speech twenty minutes ago. We need that finished. Can't start at all otherwise.
Milly Well, can't someone else . . . ?
Stewart It's all right. I'll do it, I'll do it.
Gosforth (*at the tent flap*) Oh no. Here comes the wretched rain.
Milly Oh no.

Thunder

Oh, just look at it. Nobody'll come and the ones that are here will go home.
Gosforth Dear oh dear. Like a monsoon. Hang on, I'll try raising their morale. Try and keep them here somehow. (*He snatches up the loud-hailer and stands in the doorway*) This is only a short shower. Please feel free to shelter in the main marquee. I repeat this is only a short shower. (*He lowers the loud-hailer*) I don't think that convinced anybody.
Milly (*suddenly*) Oh, heavens.
Gosforth What is it?
Milly I left the biscuits out the back . . .

Millie hurries out, after picking up a newspaper to protect her hair

Stewart sits drinking

Gosforth I wouldn't drink too much of that, Stewart old boy, if you're not used to it.
Stewart Go to hell, Gosforth, you fascist.
Gosforth Your platform's getting a bit damp out there. Want a hand to drag it in?
Stewart Go to hell, Gosforth, you swine.
Gosforth All right, I'll drag it in.

Gosforth goes out, as Milly comes in with a cardboard box of biscuits

Milly Phew! Just saved them in time. Could you give me a hand, Stewart?
Stewart . . .
Stewart Hah!
Milly Oh, well. Don't then . . .

*Milly goes out. Gosforth comes in through the other doorway, dragging
Stewart's platform. A small, square rostrum with a rail like a wayside
pulpit*

Gosforth Pity to let this get ruined. You put a lot of effort into this.
Never seen such a shower out there. The lucky-dip tub's like a water-
butt already. What was there left to do on this, Stokes? Stokes? Oh,
come on, stop sitting there feeling sorry for yourself, Stokes . . .

*Milly staggers in with a second box of biscuits, holding the wet newspaper
on her head*

Milly Could one of you give old Mr Durban a hand with the tea urn?
He seems to have got bogged down in the mud by the gate. He's stuck.
Gosforth All right, all right, I'll go. No use expecting our Boy Scout to do
anything.

Gosforth goes out through the other door

Milly Oh, Stewart, honestly, just sitting there leaving poor old Mr Durban
to cope. He's over seventy, you know—and those Wolf Cubs of yours
are throwing mud at each other. I wish you'd try and control them.
They should be taking shelter. Oh well, don't blame me if they all go
down with pneumonia.
Stewart What made you do it, Milly?
Milly What?
Stewart With a man like—Gosforth? That fascist . . .
Milly Oh, don't drag politics into it, Stewart, for goodness' sake.
Stewart What made you do it, Milly?
Milly (*brightly*) Oh, I don't know. Can't remember now.
Stewart What do you mean, you can't remember?
Milly (*taking the newspaper from her head*) Well, I suppose I can, yes. It
was while you were off at the Scout Jamboree.
Stewart Oh God . . .
Milly I went across to the pub to get some brandy—for Mother—she
thought she had a cold coming. She wanted some in her hot milk.
Stewart Go on.
Milly Well—Gordon was there, behind the bar as usual. It was a very
quiet evening for some reason. No-one in the saloon at all. He offered
to buy me a drink.
Stewart He got you drunk. (*He takes another swig*)

Milly No, he didn't. Not very, anyway. Not as drunk as you'll get if you keep going at that the way you are.

Stewart Typical. Got you drunk and then took advantage of you.

Milly Do you want to hear what happened or not?

Stewart No. Yes—I don't know.

Milly Anyway. It sort of got later—and—Mother didn't get her brandy. Gordon closed up the bar and we sat on in there talking. He told me all about his ex-wife and I talked about you.

Stewart You talked to him about me? Us?

Milly Yes.

Stewart How dare you talk to that man about us.

Milly Oh, for heaven's sake, Stewart, if you're going to be righteously indignant, do take off that stupid hat.

Stewart This is not a stupid hat.

Milly It is on you.

Stewart This is my badge of office.

Milly And those absurd baggy shorts.

Stewart You always said you liked me in my uniform . . .

Milly Well, I don't any more.

Stewart I don't know what's got into you, Milly.

Milly I don't either. I've grown up, I think. I'm thirty-four, pregnant by a man I don't much care for and I've grown up. And not before bloody time . . .

Milly goes out

Stewart stands unsteadily, adjusts his uniform and pours himself another drink

The Vicar enters holding a notice-board over his head which reads: "Grand Fête Today 2.30 p.m." In his other hand, a microphone stand

Vicar My goodness, my goodness. Ah, Stewart.

Stewart Hallo, Vicar.

Vicar You—er—heard the broadcast—I take it?

Stewart Yes. I did.

Vicar I'm sorry. Not the most tactful way to hear that sort of news.

Stewart No.

Vicar It must have come as a great shock to you.

Stewart To everyone. Everyone heard it, you know.

Vicar Ah, yes. But then everyone knew it, you see. Except you, that is.

Stewart They did?

Vicar Oh, yes.

Stewart How?

Vicar Well, it's a very small village, isn't it? And the spectacle of Miss Carter being let out at the side door of the "Fox and Hounds" at six a.m. on a Sunday morning is not all that common an occurrence.

Stewart I see.

Vicar If you hadn't been at your Jamboree, I . . . (*Holding up the mike stand*) I brought this in with me. I don't know if it's vital to anything.

Stewart Oh yes, it's the microphone stand, I think.

Vicar Ah. Well. Your Wolf Cubs appear to be rolling in the mud.

Stewart Let them. Who cares.

Vicar Well, no, they're enjoying themselves. I don't know what their mothers are going to say. All those clean white P.T. vests.

Gosforth staggers in with the tea urn, followed by Milly

Milly Can you manage?

The Vicar goes to help, but burns his hand on it

Gosforth Yes—weighs a ton . . . (*Dumping it down on the end of the table*) Right. That's it. There we are.

Milly It's a good job you rescued him. Old Mr Durban had sunk in up to his knees.

Vicar Oh dear.

Gosforth Well now. Change of plan is called for, I think—Stewart, will you lay off that stuff. I think in view of the weather an early tea is called for. Can you manage that, Milly?

Milly Yes, I think so. I've seen Mrs Winchurch around somewhere. She can help me. My other ladies weren't due till three-thirty.

Gosforth And what the hell's happened to the Hadforth Band? They should have been here half an hour ago. Right. Revised schedule of event one. Opening speech by Councillor Mrs Pearce . . .

Milly In the rain?

Gosforth She needn't get wet. We can put that platform in the tent entrance there—she can stand just inside the doorway. Anyway, even if they can't see her they can hear her. As soon as she's through—tea. Then we just pray that by the time we've finished that, this lot will have passed over. We'll have to scrub round the gym display—I don't think the instructor's quite up to it anyway.

Stewart Go to blazes, Gosforth. (*He drinks again, from the bottle*)

Gosforth And to you, old boy. Now then, let's—where the devil is she?

Milly Who?

Gosforth Councillor Mrs Pearce? Where is she? What did you do with her, Vicar?

Vicar Oh. Yes. I think I rather lost sight of her during the—broadcast. I thought she was—that's odd. Oh dear.

Gosforth (*snatching up his loud-hailer and marching to the door*) Councillor Mrs Pearce. Would Councillor Mrs Pearce kindly report to the tea tent. (*Lowering the loud-hailer*) She can't have got far.

Vicar I'll see if I can find her.

The Vicar runs out with his notice-board over his head

A big clap of thunder is heard. Gosforth starts fixing the mike into its stand which he arranges in front of the platform in the doorway. Milly starts to put out a few cups and saucers

Milly I wonder how many there's going to be of them?
Gosforth How many cups have you got there?
Milly About three hundred and fifty.
Gosforth Well, I should start with about six. (*Examining the amplifier*) My God, the rain's getting on to this thing. It'll short out completely if we're not careful. (*He moves it to the side of the table. Stewart obstructs him*) Look, Stewart, would you mind . . . Milly, will you get your boy-friend out of the road, please.
Stewart I'm not her boy-friend.
Milly He's not my boy-friend.

The Vicar returns

Vicar No sight nor sound of her. I hope she's all right.
Gosforth Where the hell has she got to? She can't have vanished into thin . . .

Mrs Pearce enters through the other door. Her feather hat is limp, her shoes and stockings coated in mud. She is exhausted and soaked

Milly stifles a scream

Gosforth Councillor Mrs Pearce!
Vicar Good heavens.
Mrs Pearce Oh. At last . . .
Vicar Do sit down, Mrs Pearce, please.
Milly What happened to you?
Mrs Pearce (*breathless*) I went—I saw your church—I thought I had time to take a quick look . . .
Vicar Yes, yes. You're very welcome to.
Mrs Pearce It started raining—I found I'd lost my sense of direction. One of your Wolf Cubs finally directed me . . .
Vicar Good boy, good boy . . .
Mrs Pearce The wrong way. I finished up in a ploughed field.
Gosforth Typical. Pack of little vandals . . . Mrs Pearce, if you're feeling up to it, I really feel we ought to start the ceremony—for what it's worth. Then we can get on with our tea.
Mrs Pearce All right.
Gosforth Feeling fit?
Mrs Pearce Yes, yes.
Gosforth Right, then. Let's get weaving. With or without the Hadforth Band, blast them. (*Switching on the amplifier*) Just pray this thing's still working.
Stewart You swine, Gosforth.
Gosforth (*ignoring Stewart*) So far so good. (*He climbs on the platform.*

He taps the mike experimentally) One—two—three—four—success. Good afternoon to you, ladies and gentlemen—boys and girls. (*Breaking off as he sights something*) Will you Wolf Cubs not persecute that pig, please. Now keep well clear of the pig—thank you. (*Resuming*) May I first of all thank you all for braving the elements this afternoon and coming along here to support this very worthwhile cause. That cause is, as we all know, the building of the new village hall. Something that eventually can be enjoyed by each and everyone of us in this community. I won't keep you longer than I have to— I'm well aware this is hardly the weather for standing about and listening to speeches. We will, in view of the circumstances, be altering our programme of events slightly. We plan to take tea in the tea tent, that is the tent from which I am speaking to you now, immediately after we have heard from our distinguished Guest of Honour. She herself needs very little introduction I am sure. Both she and her husband have both served as councillors for this ward for many years and during that time have, I feel—and here I'm speaking over and above any purely party political feeling—have, I feel, done tremendous work both for us and for that whole community to which we all belong. Without further ado, may I call upon Councillor Mrs Pearce formally to open this Grand Fête. Councillor Mrs Pearce.

Gosforth steps down to make room for Mrs Pearce. Meanwhile, under this previous speech:

Vicar (*to Milly, in a whisper*) Do you think it would be very wicked of me to sneak a cup of tea now?
Milly (*whispering*) Not at all. Help yourself.
Vicar (*whispering*) Thank you. I will.

Milly returns her attention to the speech. The Vicar goes over and takes a cup. Anxious not to get in anyone's way, he swivels the urn round so that the tap is directly over the amplifier. He turns on the tap and starts to fill his cup. Stewart, now lying on the ground, starts to sing softly

Milly (*to Stewart*) Ssh.

The Vicar, having poured his tea, finds he is unable to turn off the tap of the tea urn

Vicar Oh dear.
Milly Ssh.
Vicar Help!
Milly What?
Vicar I can't turn off the tap.
Milly Oh. Wait . . .

Milly dashes over, hands him another empty cup to catch the flow and takes the full one from him. They continue this chain of filling cups, in between time trying vainly to stem the flow of tea from the urn without success. This continues until Gosforth has finished his speech. As soon as he has done so, Mrs Pearce steps on to the rostrum

Mrs Pearce Ladies and gentlemen. I seem to have brought the wrong weather with me, I'm afraid. But this is an occurrence which I don't think for once you can blame on either me or the Conservative Party. It reminds me very much of a saying my husband is very fond of quoting. The rain in Spain may indeed fall mainly on the plain—but what's left of it seems to fall mainly in Kent. Joking apart, and I don't want to turn this into a political occasion in any way—but since we have been in control of your Council—I think everyone here will agree with me—the Conservatives have made startling progress—(*gripping the microphone*)—progress not only for the rich among you but also for the not so well off—not only for the rich man in his castle—but also for the poor man at his gate—if I may, I'd like to take a brief look at our recent record on Council Housing. Over three hundred new houses in less than two years. Compared, I may remind you, with the previous Labour best of only a hundred and fifty Council houses. In other words, a hundred per cent increase. Startling indeed . . .

Under the above:

Gosforth (*in an urgent whisper*) What the blazes are you doing?
Milly It's stuck.
Gosforth What's stuck?
Milly The tap's stuck.
Vicar Could we possibly turn it upside down?
Gosforth Why the hell don't you leave things alone?

Stewart has found the loud-hailer and begins to croon through it, softly at first, a selection of camp-fire songs

Stewart Ging gang gooly gooly gooly gooly watcha . . .
Gosforth Shut up, Stokes! Milly, get that off him.
Milly (*who is preoccupied running to and fro with cups*) How can I?
Gosforth (*wrestling with the tap*) Damn and blast this thing.
Stewart Here we sit like birds in the wilderness . . .
Milly Shut up, Stewart.
Stewart (*at Mrs Pearce*) Right-wing fascist propaganda.
Gosforth Stokes! Someone get him out of here.
Stewart Long live the Revolution!
Gosforth (*moving away from the urn*) Just a minute. Keep things going, keep things going . . .

Gosforth goes to Stewart, takes the loud-hailer off him and drags him roughly to his feet

Come on, you, come on.
Stewart Kindly do not molest me, you adulterer.
Gosforth Come on. Out in the fresh air. (*He drags Stewart to the other entrance*)
Stewart Baden-Powell for President.
Gosforth Come on.
Stewart Home Rule for Wolf Cubs.

Gosforth drags Stewart out

Milly and the Vicar continue to drain off the urn into a growing number of cups

Milly We're never going to drink all this tea.
Vicar Quickly, please, quickly.
Milly I'm being as quick as I can.

Gosforth returns, wiping his hands

Gosforth That's fixed him. Right. Next job. Now stand clear, Vicar, stand clear.
Vicar I don't think I should. I might . . .
Gosforth (*pushing him back*) Please stand clear.

Gosforth wrestles with the tap afresh. With the Vicar's cup no longer there to catch it, the tea pours into the amplifier below. There is a loud buzzing and howling noise from the loudspeaker system. Mrs Pearce, who is holding the mike and still in full flow, suddenly begins both physically and vocally to oscillate violently. Gosforth manages to turn off the urn

Done it! (*Aware of the din*) What the hell's happening?
Milly Look . . . (*She points to Mrs Pearce*)
Vicar Good gracious. (*He runs to Mrs Pearce*) Mrs Pearce . . .

The Vicar and Gosforth lever Mrs Pearce away from the mike. The Vicar grabs the stand and gets a shock

Gosforth Steady, Vicar, steady . . .

Gosforth hits the Vicar's hand from the stand, and turns in time to catch Mrs Pearce, who collapses

Give us a hand, Milly.
Milly (*going to do so*) Right.
Gosforth Are you all right, Councillor Mrs Pearce?
Mrs Pearce (*weakly quavering*) The Conservative Party have always striven . . .
Gosforth Vicar, can you and Milly lift her over to the first-aid people?
Vicar Very well, very well.
Gosforth I'll hold the fort here.
Mrs Pearce We have always believed in a fair deal for everyone . . .
Milly All right, Mrs Pearce.
Gosforth Where the hell's that bloody Hadforth Band? It's never here when you want it.

Milly and the Vicar assist Mrs Pearce towards the other exit

Vicar We'll take her to the first-aid tent.
Milly It's not up.
Gosforth Then tell them to get it up. This is an emergency.

Milly, the Vicar and Mrs Pearce go out

(*Surveying the scene for a second*) Oh dear God . . . (*He snatches up the loud-hailer and jumps on to the platform*) Ladies and gentlemen. Sorry about this. Just goes to show these little technical hitches can happen to the best of us. There's going to be another slight alteration in our schedule. In fifteen minutes, at three-fifteen, we'll be having the home-made cake judging competition in the main marquee, and after . . .

There is a loud crash

Oh my God. Now I warned you Wolf Cubs, that scaffolding was unsafe. Please stand back, everyone. Let the first-aid people through. Please stand well back . . .

There is the sound of a brass band approaching

Oh dear God, what a time to turn up. (*Through the loud-hailer again*) Hadforth Band! Hadforth Band! There are Wolf Cubs on the ground requiring minor medical attention—would you please be very careful where you march. I repeat, please be very careful where you are marching . . .

He leans on the platform rail which promptly drops away. As he falls through the tent entrance, the Lights fade to a Black-out

A TALK IN THE PARK

A park

Four park benches, separated but not too distant from each other. On one sits Beryl, a belligerent young girl at present engrossed in reading a long letter. On another sits Charles who looks what he is, a businessman dressed for the weekend. He is slowly thumbing his way through a thick report. On another sits Doreen, middle-aged, untidily dressed, feeding the birds from a bag of breadcrumbs. On the remaining bench sits Ernest, a younger man. He sits gazing into space. The birds sing. After a moment, Arthur enters. He is a bird-like man in a long mackintosh, obviously on the look-out for company. Eventually, he approaches Beryl's bench

Arthur Is this seat occupied, by any chance?
Beryl (*shortly*) No. (*She continues to read*)
Arthur Great, great. (*He sits*)

A pause. Arthur takes deep breaths and gives a few furtive glances in Beryl's direction

Student, I see?
Beryl What?
Arthur Student, I bet. You look like a student. Always tell a student.
Beryl No.
Arthur Ah. You look like one. You're young enough to be a student. Quite young enough. That's the life, isn't it? Being a student. Not a care in the world. Sitting in the park on a day like this. In the sunshine. Rare enough we see the sun, eh? Eh? Rare.
Beryl Yes. (*She refuses to be drawn into conversation*)
Arthur Mind you, I shouldn't be here. By rights, I should be at home. That's where I should be. Inside my front door. I've got plenty of things I should be doing. The kitchen shelves to name but three. Only you sit at home on a day like today. Sunday. Nothing to do. On your own—you think to yourself, this is no good, this won't get things done—and there you are talking to yourself. You know what they say about people who talk to themselves? Eh? Eh? Yes. So I thought it's outdoors for you, else they'll come and take you away. Mind you, I'm never at a loss. I'm a very fulfilled person. I have, for example, one of the biggest collections of cigarette cards of anyone alive or dead that I know of. And you don't get that by sitting on your behind all day. But I'll let you into a secret. Do you know what it is that's the most valuable thing there is you can hope to collect? People. I'm a collector of people. I look at them, I observe them, I hear them talk, I listen to their manner

of speaking and I think, hallo, here's another one. Different. Different again. Because I'll let you into a secret. They are like fingerprints. They are never quite the same. And I've met a number in my lifetime. Quite a number. Some good, some bad, all different. But the best of them, and I'm saying this to you quite frankly and openly, the best of them are women. They are superior people. They are better people. They are cleaner people. They are kinder-hearted people. If I had a choice, I'd be a woman. Now that makes you laugh, I expect, but it's the truth. When I choose to have a conversation, I can tell you it's with a woman every time. Because a woman is one of nature's listeners. Most men I wouldn't give the time of day to. Now I expect that shocks you but it's the truth. Trouble is, I don't get to meet as many women as I'd like to. My particular line of work does not bring me into contact with them as much as I would wish. Which is a pity.

Beryl gets up

Beryl Excuse me. (*She moves off*)
Arthur Are you going?

Beryl moves to Charles's bench

Beryl (*to Charles*) Excuse me, is this seat taken?
Charles (*barely glancing up*) No. (*He moves along his bench*)
Beryl (*sitting*) Thanks. Sorry, only the man over there won't stop talking. I wanted to read this in peace. I couldn't concentrate. He just kept going on and on about his collections or something. I normally don't mind too much, only if you get a letter like this, you need all your concentration. You can't have people talking in your ear—especially when you're trying to decipher writing like this. He must have been stoned out of his mind when he wrote it. It wouldn't be unusual. Look at it. He wants me to come back. Some hopes. To him. He's sorry, he didn't mean to do what he did, he won't do it again I promise, etc., etc. I seem to have heard that before. It's not the first time, I can tell you. And there's no excuse for it, is there? Violence. I mean, what am I supposed to do? Keep going back to that? Every time he loses his temper he . . . I mean, there's no excuse. A fracture, you know. It was nearly a compound fracture. That's what they told me. (*Indicating her head*) Right here. You can practically see it to this day. Two X-rays. I said to him when I got home, I said, "You bastard, you know what you did to my head?" He just stands there. The way he does. "Sorry," he says, "I'm ever so sorry." I told him. I said, "You're a bastard, that's what you are. A right, uncontrolled, violent, bad-tempered bastard." You know what he said? He says, "You call me a bastard again and I'll smash your stupid face in." That's what he says. I mean, you can't have a rational, civilized discussion with a man like that, can you? He's a right bastard. My friend Jenny, she says, "You're a looney, leave him for God's sake. You're a looney." Who needs that? You tell me one person who needs that? Only where do you go? I mean, there's all my things—my personal things. All my—everything. He's

even got my bloody Post Office book. I'll finish up back there, you wait and see. I must be out of my tiny mind. Eh. Sometimes I just want to jump down a deep hole and forget it. Only I know that bastard'll be waiting at the bottom. Waiting to thump the life out of me. Eh?

Charles Yes. Excuse me. (*He gets up*)

Beryl I'm sorry, I didn't mean to embarrass you.

Charles No, no.

Beryl I just had to . . .

Charles Quite all right. Quite all right.

Charles moves over to Doreen

(*To Doreen*) Nobody here, is there?

Doreen What?

Charles Nobody here?

Doreen Nobody where? (*She looks round*)

Charles Sitting here.

Doreen No. No.

Charles Sorry. Do you mind if I do? (*He sits*) I won't disturb you. Girl over there's got boy-friend trouble. Comes and pours it all out on me—as if I'm interested. I mean, we've all been through it at one time or another. Why she should think I should be interested. I mean, we've all got troubles no doubt. But we all don't sit on a bench and bore some poor innocent stranger to death. I mean, that in my book spells S for selfishness. And have you noticed that it's invariably the young? They think we haven't been through it. Can't imagine that perhaps we were young, too. Don't know where they think we all came from. I mean, five years ago I had a house in the country, a charming wife, two good children, couldn't imagine a happier family. My wife dies suddenly, my children can't stand the place a moment longer and emigrate to Canada so I sell the house and there I am in a flat I can hardly swing a cat in. But I don't go round boring other people with it. That's life. I've had twenty—no, more like twenty-five, good years. Who am I to complain if I get a few bad ones thrown in as well. Make no mistake, I know I'm in for some bad ones. Things are going to get worse before they get better. Bound to. And you know an interesting thing about trouble? I always think it's a bit like woodworm. Once you've got a dose, if you're not careful, it starts to spread. Starts in your family and, before you know it, it's into your business. Which explains why I'm sitting here reading a report that's been put together so badly that I've got to read it through on my one day off and condense it into another report before I can even be certain whether I'm bankrupt. I mean, I don't know if you're interested but just take a look at this page here, this is a typical page. Can you make head or tail . . .

Doreen gets up and moves away

(*Muttering*) Oh, I beg your pardon.

Doreen moves to Ernest's bench

Doreen Excuse me.
Ernest Eh?
Doreen Excuse me. May I sit here for a moment? (*She sits*) The man over there has been—you know—I didn't want to make a scene but he—you know. I mean, I suppose I should call the police—but they'd never catch him. I mean, most of the police are men as well, aren't they? Between you and me, I have heard that most of the police women are as well. Men dressed up, you know. Special Duties, so called. So my ex-husband informed me. I mean, it's terrible, you can't sit in a park these days without some men—you know—I mean, I'm on a fixed income—I don't want all that. That comes from my husband. My ex-husband. He runs a pub. In the country. But I had to leave him. We got to the stage when it was either that or—you know. I love dogs, you see, and he would never—he refused, point blank. And the day came when I knew I must have a dog. It became—you know—like an obsession. So I left. I usually have my dog here with me only he's at the vet's. He's only a puppy. They had to keep him in. He's being—you know—poor little thing. He'd have seen that man off. He's a loyal little dog. He understands every word I say to him. Every word. I said to him this morning, Ginger-boy, I said—you're coming down to the vet's with me this morning to be—you know, and his little ears pricked up and his tail wagged. He knew, you see. I think dogs are more intelligent than people. They're much better company and the wonderful thing is that once you've got a little dog, you meet other people with dogs. And what I always say is that people who have dogs they're the nicest sort of people. They're the ones I know I'd get on with.

Ernest gets up

Have you got a dog, by any chance?

Ernest ignores her and creeps behind the trees to Arthur

Ernest (*sitting down next to Arthur*) Excuse me. Just taking refuge. Nut case over there. Bloody woman prattling on about her dog. Ought to be locked up. Thinks every man's after her. I mean, look. Look at it. After her? She'd have to pay 'em. You know the sort though, don't you? If you let her talk to you long enough, she'll talk herself into thinking you've assaulted her. Before you know it, she's screaming blue murder, you'll be carried off by the fuzz and that's your lot. Two years if you're lucky. I mean, I came out here to get away from the wife. Don't want another one just like her, do I? I mean. That's why I'm in the park. Get away from the noise. You got kids? Don't have kids. Take my tip, don't get married. Looks all right, but believe me—nothing's your own. You've paid for it all but nothing's your own. Yap, yap, yap. Want, want, want. Never satisfied. I mean, no word of a lie, I look at her some mornings and I think, blimey, I must have won last prize in a raffle. Mind you, I dare say she's thinking the same. In fact, I know she is. Certainly keeps me at a distance. Hallo, dear, put your money on the table and she's off out. Don't see her for dust. Sunday mornings, it's a race to see who can get out first. Loser keeps the baby. Well, this morning I made it first. Here I am in the quiet. Got away from the noise. You know something interesting? Most of our lives are noise, aren't they? Artificial man-made noise. But you sit out here and you can listen—and—well, there's a bit of traffic but apart from that—peace. Like my mother used to say. Shut your eyes in the country and you can hear God breathing. (*He shuts his eyes*)

Arthur (*leaning across to Beryl*) Hey—hey—pssst! I've got a right one here. Thinks he's listening to God breathing . . . (*He laughs*)

Beryl (*leaning across to Charles*) He's talking again. To me. What do you do? (*She smiles*)

Charles (*leaning across to Doreen*) There she goes again. What did I tell you? Chapter Two of the boyfriend saga.

Doreen (*leaning across to Ernest*) He's talking to me. If he does it any more, I'll call the police . . .

Ernest (*to Arthur*) Oh, blimey. Why doesn't she go home? Hark at her. Can you hear her? Rabbitting on . . .

The following, final section, is played as a Round. Doreen finishes first, then Charles cuts out, followed by Beryl, Arthur, and then Ernest

Arthur (*to Beryl*) Hey—hey.

Beryl continues to ignore him

Oh, suit yourself.
Beryl (*to Charles*) Psst—psst.

Charles ignores her

Oh, be like that.
Charles (*to Doreen*) I say, I say.

Doreen ignores him

Oh, all right, don't then . . .
Doreen (*to Ernest*) Excuse me, excuse me, excuse me.

Ernest ignores her

Oh, really.
Ernest (*nudging Arthur*) Oy—oy.

Arthur ignores him

Oh, all right, then. Don't. Don't then. Might as well talk to yourself.

They all sit sulkily. The Lights fade to a Black-out, and—

the CURTAIN *falls*

Notes

(These notes are intended to serve the needs of overseas students as well as those of English-born users.)

Mother Figure

1   *dinkie* — baby-talk for a drink.
1   *toothipegs* — baby-talk for teeth.
1   *botty* — baby-talk for bottom.
3   *transfer charge call* — telephone call in which the person who receives the call agrees to pay for it.
4   *door chimes* — instead of an ordinary door-bell some houses have an instrument which, when the door-bell is pushed, produces either a sound of chiming bells or even a simple tune.
4   *pudgy* — short and fat.
5   *sotto voce* — musical term meaning 'in a quiet voice'.
5   *choccy bics* — baby-talk for chocolate biscuits.
7   *idle loafer* — workshy layabout.
10   *nutter* — colloquial for idiot or lunatic.
11   *'Georgie Porgie' etc.* — well-known children's nursery rhyme.
11   *Sleep tight . . . Hope the bugs don't bite.* — rhyme often used by parents to young children after putting them to bed.

Drinking Companion

13   *three-star hotel* — hotel offering moderate degree of luxury.
13   *muzak* — background music over loudspeakers.
13   *the ringing tone* — sound indicating that the phone is ringing out at the number you have dialled.
13   *large ones* — usually denotes a double measure of a drink.
13   *Mason's* — (fictional) local departmental store.
15   *charge it to Room two-four-nine, please* — put the costs of the drinks onto the final bill of room number 249.
16   *Playing the field* — going out with several men.
16   *Luton* — town thirty miles north of London with a reputation for being boring.
16   *Shepherd's Bush* — unfashionable district of London.

17 *En suite bathroom* — bathroom adjoining the bedroom.
18 *saloon bar* — bar open to non-residents of the hotel.
18 *foyer* — entrance and reception area of the hotel.
21 *eye to eye* — seeing things in the same way.
21 *Washout* — all the colour and brightness has gone from their lives.
22 *thick head* — a dull headache — usually as a result of heavy drinking.

Between Mouthfuls

27 *Hors d'oeuvres* — starters to a meal which sharpen the appetite.
33 *over the moon* — excited and happy.
35 *a terrific cheek* — an outrageous piece of impudence.
38 *out on my ear* — thrown out of the firm, dismissed.

Gosforth's Fête

40 *fête* — a fund-raising event run by volunteers and consisting of side shows, displays, refreshments, etc.
40 *jerry-rigged* — hastily and not very securely put together.
40 *behindhand* — behind schedule.
41 *Wolf Cubs* — Junior section of the Boy Scout movement, for boys aged 8—11 years.
41 *P.T. display* — display of Physical Training exercises.
41 *thick as two planks* — very unintelligent.
41 *bettery-operated loudhailer* — cone-shaped instrument which amplifies the voice; it is held up to the speaker's mouth.
42 *guy-rope crisis* — problems with the ropes that hold the tents up.
42 *sash cord* — old window frames work on a counter-balance system involving ropes and pulleys. The ropes are known as sash cords.
42 *kick-off* — sporting term meaning the beginning — particularly in football.
42 *bowling for the pig* — game of skittles in which the competitor with the largest score is awarded a pig as a prize.
42 *local quack* — colloquialism for local doctor.
44 *lovey* — general term of endearment.
44 *old girl* — another term of general endearment.
46 *Brownies* — Junior section of the Girl Guide movement, for girls aged 8—11 years.
46 *spinster of this parish* — term used in the marriage ceremony

to refer to the bride prior to marriage and which assumes her
virginity.

47 *swiped* — stolen.

48 *pneumonia* — disease of the lungs and respiratory tracts —
associated with getting wet through.

48 *Scout Jamboree* — meeting of scouts from several areas —
usually at a central camp over three or four days.

51 *Let's get weaving* — let us begin.

53 *Conservative Party* — the right-wing political party.

53 *The rain in Spain* etc. — parody of the first line of a song from
My Fair Lady based on *Pygmalion* by G.B. Shaw.

53 *The rich man in his castle* etc. — lines from a popular English
hymn *All Things Bright and Beautiful.*

53 *What the blazes* — 'What the hell' or 'What on earth'. Linked
with the flames of hell.

53 *Ging gang gooly* etc. — well-known song by scouts round the
camp fire.

53 *Baden-Powell* — founder of the Boy Scout movement.

A Talk in the Park

56 *collections of cigarette cards* — in the 1930s and 1940s packets
of cigarettes contained picture cards of trains, famous footballers
etc., which were collected and stuck into albums.

57 *looney* — lunatic.

58 *hardly swing a cat in* — colloquial description of a small space.

59 *the fuzz* — colloquial for the police.

60 *played as a Round* — a musical form in which the singers
repeat the same phrase over and over again in counterpoint with
each other.

METHUEN STUDENT EDITIONS

☐ SERJEANT MUSGRAVE'S DANCE	John Arden	£6.99
☐ CONFUSIONS	Alan Ayckbourn	£5.99
☐ THE ROVER	Aphra Behn	£5.99
☐ LEAR	Edward Bond	£6.99
☐ THE CAUCASIAN CHALK CIRCLE	Bertolt Brecht	£6.99
☐ MOTHER COURAGE AND HER CHILDREN	Bertolt Brecht	£6.99
☐ THE CHERRY ORCHARD	Anton Chekhov	£5.99
☐ TOP GIRLS	Caryl Churchill	£6.99
☐ A TASTE OF HONEY	Shelagh Delaney	£6.99
☐ STRIFE	John Galsworthy	£5.99
☐ ACROSS OKA	Robert Holman	£5.99
☐ A DOLL'S HOUSE	Henrik Ibsen	£5.99
☐ MY MOTHER SAID I NEVER SHOULD	Charlotte Keatley	£6.99
☐ DREAMS OF ANNE FRANK	Bernard Kops	£5.99
☐ BLOOD WEDDING	Federico García Lorca	£5.99
☐ THE HOUSE OF BERNARDA ALBA	Federico García Lorca	£7.99
☐ THE MALCONTENT	John Marston	£5.99
☐ BLOOD BROTHERS	Willy Russell	£6.99
☐ DEATH AND THE KING'S HORSEMAN	Wole Soyinka	£6.99
☐ THE PLAYBOY OF THE WESTERN WORLD	J.M. Synge	£5.99
☐ OUR COUNTRY'S GOOD	Timberlake Wertenbaker	£6.99
☐ THE IMPORTANCE OF BEING EARNEST	Oscar Wilde	£5.99
☐ A STREETCAR NAMED DESIRE	Tennessee Williams	£5.99

• All Methuen Drama books are available through mail order or from your local bookshop.

Please send cheque/eurocheque/postal order (sterling only) Access, Visa, Mastercard, Diners Card, Switch or Amex.

☐☐☐☐☐☐☐☐☐☐☐☐☐☐

Expiry Date: _____ Signature: _____

Please allow 75 pence per book for post and packing U.K.
Overseas customers please allow £1.00 per copy for post and packing.

ALL ORDERS TO:

Methuen Books, Books by Post, TBS Limited, The Book Service, Colchester Road, Frating Green, Colchester, Essex CO7 7DW.

NAME: _____

ADDRESS: _____

_____

_____

Please allow 28 days for delivery. Please tick box if you do not wish to receive any additional information   ☐

Prices and availability subject to change without notice.